BENEATH
THE BULL RING

The Archaeology of Life and Death in Early Birmingham

BENEATH
THE BULL RING

*The Archaeology of Life and
Death in Early Birmingham*

Simon Buteux

BREWIN BOOKS

First published by
Brewin Books Ltd, 56 Alcester Road,
Studley, Warwickshire B80 7LG in 2003
www.brewinbooks.com

ISBN 1 85858 242 3

A Cataloguing in Publication Record
for this title is available from the British Library.

Typeset in Times
Made & Printed in Great Britain

Contents

Excavation of a 17th-century chair on the Park Street site.

Foreword

by the Leader of Birmingham City Council

'Forward' is Birmingham's motto and it aptly describes how the city has always been a place of progress and change. The new Bullring is part of Birmingham's Renaissance over the closing years of the 20th century and the opening years of the 21st. However, major developments are not new to the city centre – even before the 1960s Bull Ring our Victorian forefathers undertook massive new development in the 19th century such as the Town Hall and Corporation Street, and in the 18th century squares were laid out.

The archaeological excavations at the Bull Ring take us back even further in time and provide remarkable details about life and work in the historic heart of Birmingham hundreds of years ago. They show us how Birmingham's first entrepreneurs, the medieval lords of the manor, had the foresight to establish a market and to encourage industries such as metalworking, leather tanning and pottery making. They were themselves involved in a major redevelopment which included laying out two new roads across what had been their deer park.

The Bull Ring excavations not only demonstrated the wealth of surviving remains of the city's past but also how they can be properly investigated without holding up or preventing new development. The Birmingham Alliance has enthusiastically embraced the integration of archaeology with new development to the benefit of the people of Birmingham, adding value to their development by increasing public interest and appreciation and setting a fine example for other developers to follow. This has been achieved through the development partnership fostered by the City Council, working together with developers and their agents, which promotes quality development that the people of Birmingham can own and be proud of. This includes making sure that while we are building a new Birmingham remains of the city's past are not swept away without record.

In the Bull Ring the City Council's aims of encouraging major, high-quality development and at the same time safeguarding the city's past have come together. The Bull Ring shows how archaeological work will be successfully achieved in future developments in the city centre and elsewhere in Birmingham to the benefit of developers and the citizens of Birmingham.

Councillor Sir Albert Bore, Leader, Birmingham City Council

Foreword

by The Birmingham Alliance

ᵀᴴᴱBIRMINGHAMALLIANCE

Throughout history Birmingham has been a leading centre of trade and market innovation. One of its earliest known transformations, in the 1100s, turned it from a village into a thriving market town. Later, in the 18th century, it was described as 'the first manufacturing town in the world' and in the 19th century its industrial greatness earned it the soubriquet 'the city of a thousand trades'. In the 1960s it became one of the country's most celebrated examples of revolutionary urban planning, which brought with it the opening of the old Bull Ring shopping centre. At the time, it was one of the world's largest shopping centres outside America and an examplar of shopping centre design.

Today Birmingham is undergoing yet another transformation. The city is seeing billions of pounds of new investment, and the opening of the new 110,000m² Bullring in September 2003 is a major milestone in reviving the city's status as a leading European retail capital.

The opening of Bullring will bring over 140 retailers together in a new central focus of shopping, leisure and entertainment. Its creation will be part of a long continuum of Birmingham's history as a major trading centre. Not only has the archaeological work confirmed the site as the historic heart of the city – but through Bullring it will continue to be so.

Sited beneath the spire of St Martin's Church, this historic centre for market trading began life in 1166 when the city was awarded a charter giving it the right to have its own market. Since then, the site's existence as a market has continued to the present day. The opening of the old Bull Ring shopping centre in 1964 brought the location international prestige as one of Europe's largest and most modern shopping complexes. Almost forty years on, the 26-acre site is again the centre of innovation, this time as the home of the largest retail-led urban regeneration project in Europe: Bullring.

The construction of this latest manifestation of Birmingham's transformation has brought startling and exciting discoveries. New evidence, unearthed during archaeological digs commissioned by The Birmingham Alliance over three and a half years as part of Bullring's regeneration, has challenged established thinking about the City's prominence in medieval times.

Archaeological finds have revealed that Birmingham was a thriving industrial centre – with an important central tanning industry in the 13th and 14th centuries – long before the industrial revolution, the accepted catalyst for the city's evolution into the 'Workshop of the World'.

Numerous other finds on the Bullring site have shown, amongst other things, evidence of early town planning in the 13th and 14th centuries, and that part of a medieval deer park was sacrificed to accommodate the growing population of this flourishing urban centre. Space, it seems, was already at a premium in the 13th century.

The Birmingham Alliance is privileged to have been part of the process which has allowed so much more knowledge of the city's history to become known. The dedication of the team of archaeologists from Birmingham University during their time of discovery has been outstanding. Special thanks must be made to Mike Hodder, Birmingham City Council's planning archaeologist, Canon Adrian Newman of St Martin's-in-the-Bull Ring church and also to Cathy Mould, of CgMs Consulting, the archaeological consultant to The Birmingham Alliance. It is their efforts which have brought about this book – another vital chapter in Birmingham's fascinating history.

Jon Emery, Hammerson; Neil Varnham, Henderson Global Investors; Bob de Barr, Land Securities (Directors of The Birmingham Alliance)

Acknowledgements

This book is based almost entirely on the work of others. I am grateful to the directors of the excavations which form the basis of this book – Cathy Mould at Edgbaston Street and Moor Street, Bob Burrows and Helen Martin at Park Street, Richard Cherrington at St. Martin's Churchyard and Chris Patrick at the Birmingham Moat – for allowing me to use the results of their work prior to full publication. The full details of the excavations will be published in 2004 in two monographs, 'The Bull Ring Uncovered' and 'St. Martin's Uncovered'. I have also relied heavily on the various specialist analyses and reports which will be published in the monographs. These are: pottery – Stephanie Rátkai; small finds – Lynne Bevan; metal working debris – Matthew Nicholas; human bone – Megan Brickley, Helena Berry and Gaynor Western (St. Martin's) and Rachel Ives (Park Street); plant remains – Marina Ciaraldi; pollen – James Greig; insect remains – David Smith; animal bones – Ian Baxter; coffin wood – Rowena Gale; coffin furniture – Emma Hancox; textiles – Penelope Walton Rogers; tile and leather – Erica Macey; glass from Edgbaston Street – David Orton; dentures – Annette Hancocks; and documentary research on individuals from St. Martin's Churchyard – Jo Adams.

Managing the excavation and post-excavation phases of the work was a major task, and was carried out by Cathy Mould, Iain Ferris, Gary Coates and Annette Hancocks. The line illustrations are the work of Nigel Dodds, John Halsted and Bryony Ryder. The studio photography of pottery and other finds was carried out by Graham Norrie. Those archaeologists who contributed in various ways to the excavation and post-excavation work are too numerous to mention individually but their work is gratefully acknowledged.

The archaeological investigations 'beneath the Bull Ring' were funded by *The Birmingham Alliance*, a partnership between Hammerson, Henderson Global Investors and Land Securities, the developers of Bullring. Sincere thanks are due to all at the Alliance who ensured that the archaeological work was smoothly integrated into the pre-construction programme.

The archaeological work was carried out by the Birmingham University Field Archaeology Unit, now *Birmingham Archaeology*, a division of the Institute of Archaeology and Antiquity at the University of Birmingham. The Park Street and St. Martin's excavations were managed for the Alliance by *CgMs Consulting*. The work was facilitated by the cooperation and support of the developers, their agents and contractors. The archaeological team would especially like to thank Mel Evans, Vic Michel and Simon Wallis at the Alliance, Sara Boonham at Gardiner & Theobald, Kimber Heath at Benoy Architects, Mike Nisbet at Gardiner & Theobald

Management Services, Astorre Marinoni at Waterman Partnership, the Site Managers at Balfour Beatty Construction, Controlled Demolition, Shepherd Construction, Sir Robert McAlpine and the drivers at St. Clements Plant Hire. Special thanks are also due Canon Adrian Newman and the team from St. Martin's-in-the-Bull Ring.

Particular thanks are due to Dr Mike Hodder, Planning Archaeologist, Birmingham City Council. His tireless enthusiasm in promoting the City's archaeology has been the major factor in the successful completion of the work.

Several people kindly read drafts of this book in whole and in part. These were Steve Litherland, Cathy Mould, Mike Hodder, Richard Holt, Stephanie Rátkai, Bryony Ryder, Megan Brickley, Jo Adams, Richard Cherrington and Rebecca Hardy. Their corrections and often detailed comments and suggestions improved the book immensely. The errors and faults that remain are entirely the responsibility of the principal author. Chapter 10, 'A Mirror to Life: Analysis of the Human Remains', was written by Megan Brickley. Chapter 4, 'A Portrait of Medieval Birmingham', was substantially written by Steve Litherland and Chapter 11 'Birmingham Lives' by Jo Adams. The accounts in Chapter 8, 'Graves and Tombs: the Archaeology of St. Martin's Churchyard', and Chapter 9, 'Dear Departed: the Funerary Trade in Birmingham', draw heavily on research carried out by Richard Cherrington. Bryony Ryder and John Halsted prepared the illustrations for publication.

Alan Brewin, Alistair Brewin and the staff of Brewin Books are to be thanked for printing and publishing the book to a very short timetable.

The four excavations described in this book were the first major archaeological investigations to be carried out in Birmingham city centre. Very many people contributed to making the excavations a success. It is hoped this book does some justice to their efforts.

Illustration credits

The Birmingham Alliance kindly supplied the photographs of Bullring used on the cover and in Chapters 1 and 11. We are grateful to Myra Dean for providing the photographs of the Bull Ring area in the 1960s used in Chapters 2 and 7. The diagram in Chapter 1 showing roads centred on Birmingham is redrawn after a diagram by Victor Skipp. The plan of Birmingham in the 12th century in Chapter 1 is redrawn, with alterations, from an original by George Demidowicz. The photograph in Chapter 1 of the masonry uncovered at the site of the Birmingham Moat is reproduced from Lorna Watts, 'Birmingham Moat: its history, topography and destruction' *Transactions of the Birmingham and Warwickshire Archaeological Society* Vo. 89. The painting of the 'old knight' in Chapter 4 is by Bryony Ryder. The sketches of the crucibles in Chapter 6 are by Matthew Nicholas. Dr Nigel Baker's transcription and interpretation of Bradford's 1751 map of Birmingham is used as a base for the maps in Chapters 3 and 4.

For Becky and Tom

Chapter 1

Foundations

The Bull Ring development was a commercial venture. The aim was to invest money in order to make money. Permission was sought and money was spent to create a new market and its infrastructure. Traders would be attracted – enticed – to set up shop in the market. Substantial rents could be charged for prime locations in the market. These rents would be the return on the investment. The traders would profit too and from miles around people would come to buy whatever they wanted – the latest fashions, food and drink and other commodities – or just browse and enjoy the experience, perhaps taking

The 21st-century Bullring, with the spire of St. Martin's Church.

in a meal and some entertainment. There would be something for everyone. In the middle of the market is a church, St. Martin's, a reminder of less earthly concerns.

The words above serve to describe two events – and two visions – separated by about 830 years. The most recent of these events is the creation of a new shopping destination 'Bullring' by The Birmingham Alliance. Permissions were obtained from Birmingham City Council. The anchor stores are Selfridges and Debenhams with over 140 other shops.

The more distant of the two events took place in 1166. The developer was Peter de Birmingham, the lord of the manor. In 1166 he obtained a royal charter from King Henry II to hold a market at his '*castrum* of Birmingham'. The market was probably held in a triangular market place (which centuries later came to be known as the Bull Ring) just to the north of his residence, with a planned settlement newly laid out along its sides. The traders were the likes of butchers, mercers, tanners, dyers, metalworkers and potters. A stone church, St. Martin's, was built within the market place. The result cannot be seen today (nothing, for example, now remains to be seen of the fabric of the original church) and can only be reconstructed from scant historical sources and the findings of archaeological excavation; it is, literally, beneath the Bull Ring.

The similarity between the two events is significant – enterprise, trade and manufacture have been at the heart of Birmingham's story from 1166 to the present. But both accounts are greatly simplified, and in the case of the founding of Birmingham's first market, very little is quite certain or beyond debate. Importantly, neither the Bullring development of the 21st century nor that of the 12th century took place in a vacuum. They had to take account of what was there before and use this to best advantage.

Before the Bull Ring

There is very little direct evidence of what Birmingham was like before Peter de Birmingham bought his market charter in 1166. Clearly Peter had some sort of fortified residence or small castle here (this is our modern interpretation of the medieval term *castrum*) – the Latin charter tells us this much. This 'castle' is likely to have been on the site of the Birmingham Moat (or the 'Lord of the Manor's Moat'), which was a prominent feature on the southern edge of Birmingham until it was infilled and built over in the early 19th century. We are lucky in that this moat is depicted on early maps and views of Birmingham. One of the earliest, and a particularly good example, is William Westley's map of Birmingham in 1731. Here we see a large oval water-filled moat surrounding a cluster of buildings and garden plots. Conveniently, Westley has written inside it 'The Ancient Seat of the Lord of Birmingham'. Just to the northwest of the moat we see St. Martin's Church sitting within a still recognisable triangular market place, although somewhat encroached upon by buildings. Significantly, however, the entrance to the moat, flanked by what look like two towers or gatehouses, does not open towards the church or market place; rather it faces eastwards, looking down what is now Digbeth to the crossing of the River Rea. To the south of the moat the land is not built up, even in the 18th century, but is a pattern of fields, lanes and watercourses.

Therefore, Peter de Birmingham's castle once stood in what was essentially a rural landscape. We do not know exactly when it was built, but it may not have been that much before 1166. It was strategically located, however, overlooking the valley of the River Rea and the important crossing of the river at the foot of Digbeth. Digbeth itself is likely to be an ancient road, predating the castle and the town. From the south and east roads approached the Rea crossing from Alcester, Stratford, Warwick and Coventry. Joined together at the Rea crossing the road became a major thoroughfare (in 12th-century terms) and climbed up Digbeth towards the Birmingham ridge, where the roads fanned out again, to Lichfield, Stafford, Wolverhampton, Dudley, Halesowen and Worcester. Here was a good place to plant a castle – and a market. However, we do not know precisely which of these roads followed routes which predate the creation of the market and which were created

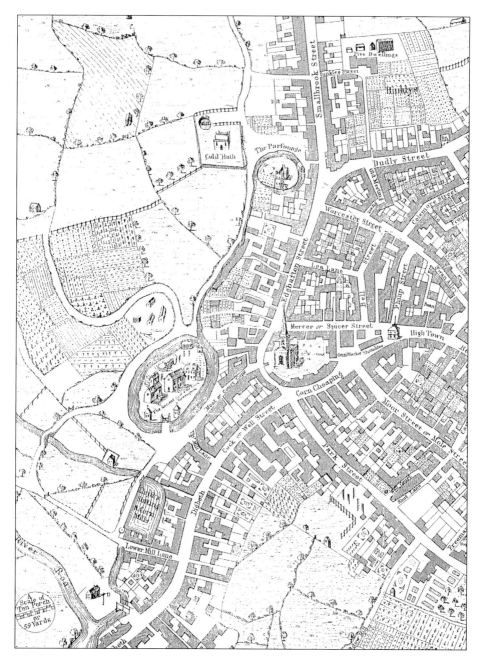

Part of William Westley's map of 1731, the first map of Birmingham. The Lord of the Manor's Moat (Birmingham Moat) and the Parsonage Moat were still extant at this time. The map is drawn with north to the right.

later or diverted to take advantage of the market; like the developers of the 21st-century Bullring, Peter had to have an eye to his infrastructure.

Nor do we know exactly what Peter de Birmingham's castle looked like. Archaeological investigations were carried out on the site in the 1970s during redevelopment of Smithfield Market. However, the amount of later disturbance had been very severe and the planning conditions at the time did not allow the archaeologists to do a proper excavation. All that was allowed to the archaeologists was to observe the building contractors' works and carry out small-scale excavation and recording when and where it was convenient for the contractors. Nevertheless, a section of finely chamfered medieval sandstone walling was uncovered, which indicated a building of some pretension, and stone mouldings were uncovered which, on the grounds of parallels with stonework from Sandwell Priory, are likely to date to the 12th century. So, around the time Peter bought his market charter he appears to have built – or rebuilt – his manor house in stone.

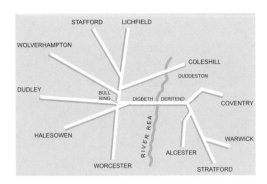

Diagram showing medieval roads centred on Birmingham. The Bull Ring was the focus for these roads, with traffic from the east channelled up Digbeth.

Part of a medieval stone building revealed on the site of the Birmingham Moat during redevelopment of Smithfield Market in the 1970s.

The moat which survived down to the 19th century may have been a 12th century feature also. Further observation and recording of a section of the moat in Upper Dean Street was possible in 2000 during the Bullring redevelopment; pottery recovered from the earliest silting within the moat dated exclusively to the medieval period. Furthermore, the circular form of the moat suggests an 11th- or 12th-century date; moats of the 13th and 14th centuries tended to be square. A survey of the town of 1529 shows that at that time the moat was still crossed by means of a drawbridge, although the medieval manor house was said to be ruinous; a mansion was built on the site later in the 16th century. Within the moat outbuildings such as kitchens, stables and stores would have stood, in addition to the manor house.

In addition to a strategic location, another important consideration in the siting of a castle was the provision of water. The water supply to Birmingham in medieval times was a consequence of geology. The Birmingham Moat sat directly over a geological fault that divides water-bearing sandstone from impervious Mercia Mudstone. The harder sandstone underlies a prominent ridge about 1.2km wide that runs roughly southwest to northeast. The geological fault line largely mirrors the alignment of this ridge, but is positioned on a slightly lower contour to the southeast of the summit (upon which buildings such as St. Philip's Cathedral or the Rotunda now sit). From here the land slopes down steeply into the valley of the River Rea. Springs rise along the fault line and the water forms small rivulets, generally flowing down the slope to eventually join the River Rea. While these rivulets were never sufficiently strong enough to power heavy machinery they would have been sufficient for the needs of a host of other industrial processes – such as hemp retting, tanning, dyeing or smithing – and, moreover, near to where they issued from the sandstone they would have been relatively clean and uncontaminated. So, as we shall see, these rivulets, suitably modified and canalised, played a major role in the development of the medieval town.

The Birmingham Moat does not stand alone. As can be seen on Westley's map of 1731 there was a second, smaller moat to the west of the Birmingham Moat, known as the Parsonage Moat. It too disappeared in the early years of the 19th century. The water in the Parsonage Moat was presumably supplied by the springs, possibly from the nearby Lady Well, and then it flowed eastwards down a watercourse to feed into the Birmingham Moat. For many years, right up until the 18th century, this watercourse marked the southern boundary of the built-up area of Birmingham. It also has an important part to play in the story of Birmingham's early development. Quite what the relationship between the two moated sites was is unknown; perhaps one was the manor, the other maybe its 'home farm' (both moats have the circular form generally associated with an early date).

A further important consideration for a medieval lord was parkland, for hunting. There were two parks adjacent to the Birmingham Moat. To the south was Holme Park; and to the north, over on the other side of Digbeth, was Little Park, or Over Park as it was sometimes called.

So, from a few scraps of historical and archaeological evidence, maps and a consideration of the topography of the area we have created a picture of Birmingham before the Bull Ring. There, perched on the southern face of the sandstone ridge overlooking the Rea valley, was Peter de Birmingham's castle and manorial seat. The second moated site – the Parsonage Moat – may also have been in existence at this time. Up the hill from the crossing of the River ran an important road, Digbeth, bringing traffic from the south and east. At the top of the hill, near the castle, the roads fanned out again, heading for points north and west. All around was parkland, farmland, woodland, grazing; an organised rural landscape. But so far we have evaded an important question – was there not also a settlement, a village, a market, a nascent town even? The answer is yes, of course there was a settlement – Birmingham – but we know very little about it.

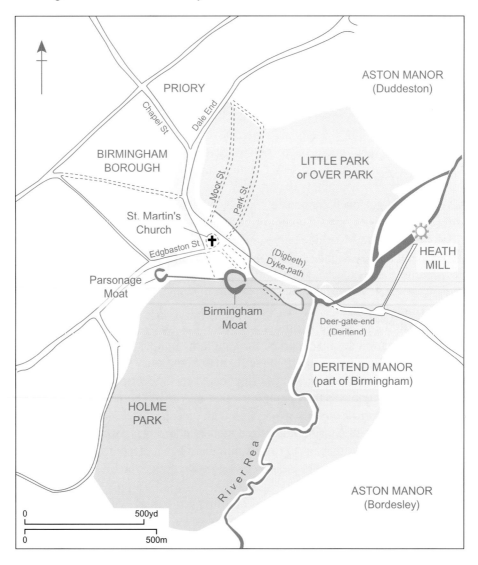

A conjectural plan of Birmingham shortly after 1166 when the market charter was obtained. Moor Street and Park Street were probably later additions to the plan of the town, in the 13th century. Built-up areas are shown in a darker tone.

Birmingham in the Domesday Book

The name 'Birmingham' means something like 'settlement (*ham*) of the followers (*inga*) of a man called *Beorma*'. The name probably dates to before AD700, and Beorma and his followers were Anglo Saxons. However, knowing that it must have existed is about all that we know about Anglo-Saxon Birmingham.

The Domesday Book of 1086 is the first documentary source to actually mention Birmingham. It was commissioned by William the Conqueror who had, of course, in 1066 replaced Anglo-Saxon rule in England with Norman rule. The Domesday Book is essentially a survey – for taxation purposes – of land ownership, land use and land value. Translated into modern English, the relevant entry reads:

> '*Richard holds of William four hides in Birmingham. Land for six ploughs; one is in the lordship. There are five villagers and four smallholders, with two ploughs. Woodland half a mile long and two furlongs wide. It was and is worth 20s. Wulfine held it freely.*'

Richard was Birmingham's first Norman lord, and the ancestor of the Peter de Birmingham who obtained his market charter in 1166; Wulfine was his Saxon predecessor before the Norman Conquest. The William referred to is William Fitz Ansculf, a powerful man with his seat at Dudley Castle. The statement of the number of inhabitants should not be taken at face value – it refers to heads of households rather than total population – but Birmingham was clearly not large, perhaps 50 persons or so. Famously, the manor was only valued at £1, an estimate of amount of rent the whole estate could be expected to bring in in a year. Even in 11th-century terms this was not much; the neighbouring manors of Aston and Handsworth, for example, were valued at £5 each.

The foundation of the market town

So, together with Peter de Birmingham's castle, the river crossing, the roads and the lord's hunting parks, we can add to our picture of Birmingham before the Bull Ring a small village. Historians have long argued about the status of this village before 1166 when Peter obtained his market charter. Had it already developed an informal market and was on the way to becoming a market town, with Peter only legalising this development by the purchase of a market charter? Or was the market town a new foundation, deliberately established and laid out by Peter? And if so, was it developed on the site of the old village or did Peter choose a new site for it, making it what historians call a 'planted town'?

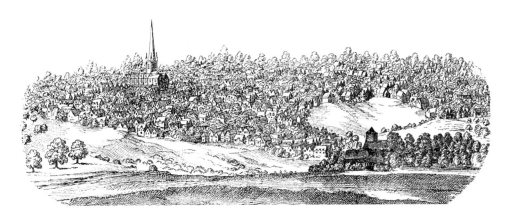

A view of Birmingham from Dugdale's Antiquities of Warwickshire, 1656. The town, viewed from the south, has not changed that much from the medieval period, and is dominated by St. Martin's Church. Holme Park is in the foreground, with the crossing of the River Rea towards the bottom right. Tightly-packed timber-framed buildings climb up Digbeth towards the church. Note how the area to the north of the church is undeveloped and shown as wooded.

Due to their large scale, the recent Bull Ring excavations have contributed to this debate. They comprised four major sites clustering around the medieval market place and produced thousands of sherds of medieval pottery (and even some Roman pottery and prehistoric flints), but not one sherd of Anglo-Saxon pottery was found nor indeed any pottery dating to before the 12th century when the market charter was obtained. Perhaps that was just bad luck; it is possible but would seem to be stretching a point. The absence of anything dating earlier strongly suggests that the market town did not develop before the 12th century and, furthermore, that it was developed on what we would today call a 'greenfield' site, some distance from the existing village.

This, in turn, strengthens the argument that the foundation of a market town at Birmingham was a deliberate speculative enterprise by its lord, Peter de Birmingham. Indeed, he may have provided his new town with a stone church at this time, sited in the middle of the triangular market place – when St. Martin's was rebuilt in 1872 it is reported that Norman stonework was found, which is most likely to be 12th century. So the market town with its stone castle or manor house and stone church may all be part of one grand conception. Whatever the case, the real story of Birmingham – the story of the transformation of an insignificant village into a great town and then a city – begins here. The archaeological excavations undertaken as part of the creation of Bullring have given a new perspective to that story.

Chapter 2

Exploring the Bull Ring

The Bull Ring excavations of 1997 to 2001 were the first major archaeological excavations to take place in Birmingham city centre. The big 'lost opportunity' was the Bull Ring redevelopment of 1961 to 1963, but at that time the archaeological profession was in a fledgling state and there were few professional archaeologists other than those teaching in universities. By the time that archaeologists had appreciated the extent of destruction of archaeological remains caused by city centre redevelopment across the country and had begun to do something effective about it – through the 'Rescue' movement which gathered pace in the 1970s – it was already too late for the Bull Ring.

When the Bull Ring came up for redevelopment again in the 1990s the situation had improved dramatically. In 1990 the government had introduced new planning guidance which stressed that archaeological remains were a 'material consideration' in the planning process. Birmingham City Council appointed an energetic Planning Archaeologist, Dr Mike Hodder, and through his advice an archaeological component was built into many development projects. A forward-looking city council itself commissioned archaeological assessments as part of its own plans for urban regeneration.

Archaeological assessments do not generally involve digging. Using historical sources, maps and on-the-ground inspection, a picture is built up of where archaeological remains might survive and what they might consist of. Thus the first stage of the archaeological work in advance of the redevelopment of the Bull Ring area was a series of archaeological assessments. Following a brief from the City Council, the assessments were commissioned by the developers of Bullring, The Birmingham Alliance. They were carried out by staff of the University of Birmingham's Birmingham Archaeology and by Cathy Mould of the Alliance's archaeological consultants, CgMs Limited.

Surely nothing can have survived?

One would imagine, looking at the centre of Birmingham today, that nothing much from earlier than the 19th century could have survived. Indeed, a great deal has been lost forever. In the area of the 1960s Bull Ring Centre, for example, it was clear that all traces of earlier remains would have been dug away. But remarkably, the detailed archaeological assessments that were carried out suggested a potential for the survival of archaeological remains over quite a wide area.

The Bull Ring area in the 1960s. The St. Martin's Circus Queensway and the Open Markets are in the middle ground, with the Bull Ring Centre to the right. Archaeological assessment and trial trenching showed that no significant remains had survived the construction of the 1960s Bull Ring Centre and Open Markets.

The next stage of the archaeological work was to test that potential. This was done by trial trenching. The Bullring redevelopment was a huge and complicated undertaking, involving the acquisition of many different parcels of land around the old triangular market place – the 21st-century shopping complex is more extensive than its 1960s predecessor – and demolition and site clearance prior to new building. Different stages of the development were spread over several years, and trial trenching by the archaeologists was programmed into the demolition and site clearance programme at each stage.

The trial trenches were dug by a mechanical excavator under close archaeological supervision. Once the excavator had cut through and removed the modern debris, the archaeologists cleaned up each trench by hand, recording and sample excavating any archaeological remains that had survived. Sometimes the trial trenches drew a blank – this was to be expected. In the area of Manzoni

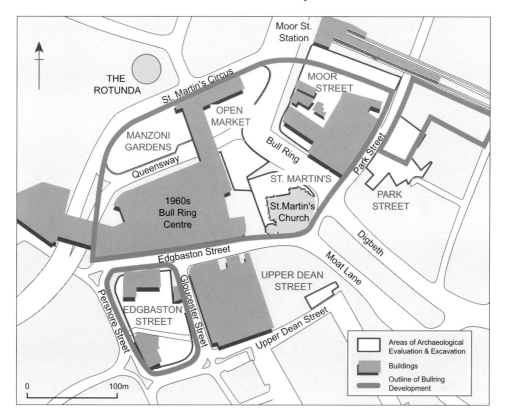

Areas of archaeological assessment, evaluation and excavation in advance of the construction of Bullring. Only in the areas of Manzoni Gardens and the Open Market did no significant archaeological remains survive.

Gardens and the Open Market, for example, nothing of archaeological significance survived. Elsewhere, however, and particularly in areas of old medieval plots to the rear of Edgbaston Street, Moor Street and Park Street, the trial trenches turned up the goods. This set in motion the third stage of the archaeological investigations, large-scale 'open area' excavations of areas that had been shown by the trial trenching to have surviving archaeological remains. These larger scale excavations generally followed fairly closely on the heels of the trial trenching.

The archaeological investigations in advance of the new Bullring were thus carried out as part of a carefully programmed and systematic three-stage process. The first stage was the 'desk-top' **assessment** of the various sites. The second stage, where merited by the results of the assessment, was the **evaluation** of the sites by means of trial trenching. The third stage, where evaluation had demonstrated the survival of significant archaeological remains, was open area **excavation.**

It will be seen how each stage progressively narrows the focus of the archaeological investigations, closing in on the target areas of archaeological survival. The approach has two major benefits. First, even in an area as large as that covered by the Bullring redevelopment, and an area that has seen so much destructive development over the years, it is possible to search out the zones

Archaeological evaluation at the Moor Street site in 2000, following demolition of modern buildings. Despite the apparent devastation, trial trenching showed that important archaeological remains dating from the 12th century survived on part of this site.

of archaeological survival. Second, the process, because carefully programmed and planned, can be carried out without unnecessary expense or disruption to the development programme.

Excavation is not the end of the story, however. There is an essential fourth stage to the process, which is often overlooked by those not familiar with archaeology. At the completion of a large excavation the archaeologists come off site having collected hundreds of finds in a variety of materials, thousands of sherds of pottery and fragments animal bone, and numerous samples of plant remains, pollen, insects and industrial residues. They have also generated a mass of written records, drawings and photographs which describe what was found – each wall, each pit, each layer of soil is individually recorded, together with its position in the stratigraphic sequence on the site and the location of the finds and samples. The fourth stage – called **post-excavation analysis** in the jargon – is to make sense of the mass of data. This is often the hardest part. Individual specialists will study the finds, pottery, bones and samples. This is time consuming and painstaking work, often taking months or years, but we will see in the chapters that follow just how much can be learned from such detailed scientific analysis.

Following the completion of an excavation a great deal of analytical work remains to be done. Here archaeologists are studying charred plant remains.

Finally, all this evidence has to be presented in detail and interpreted in a technical monograph – only then is the archaeological work considered complete. Two monographs are being produced about the Bull Ring excavations, one on the excavations at Edgbaston Street, Moor Street and Park Street, and one on the excavations in St. Martin's Churchyard. The aim of this short book is to summarise the results for a wider audience and also give a bit of explanation as to how those results were achieved.

Chapter 3

The Bull Ring Puzzle

All the effort of systematic archaeological assessment and evaluation described in the previous chapter paid off. Three main areas with remains dating back to the period when Birmingham was just a small medieval market town were identified. These areas were located amongst the burgage plots (medieval property plots) to the rear of Edgbaston Street, Moor Street and Park Street, collectively called the Bull Ring sites. The remains uncovered did not always look like much, sometimes just a few pits and ditches, and almost everywhere remains of earlier periods had been disturbed by remains of later periods.

A favourite metaphor of archaeologists is that of the jigsaw puzzle, but one that has to be done without much help from a picture on the box, and one that has most of the pieces missing. If we imagine the Bull Ring area of Birmingham in the medieval period as a jigsaw puzzle, then the picture on the box is not entirely blank; we have a sketchy outline to go on – a conjectural plan of the town worked out from historical maps and records. (It must be stressed just how conjectural this sketchy plan is; we have no detailed maps of Birmingham before the 18th century and our picture of the probable layout of the medieval town must be worked out by arguing back from these.) Also, as a consequence, we know roughly where the pieces go. However, we have just three pieces of different sizes – the Edgbaston Street, Moor Street and Park Street sites – plus a few scraps. To make matters worse, the pieces are in a bit of a mess – they are scratched, defaced and full of holes. Nevertheless on each piece can be made out numerous small details, the only spots of colour within the outline. Sometimes these details are expected – they fit the outline – at other times, as we shall see, they are unexpected.

Our job as archaeologists is to scrutinise each piece and extract as much information as we can. Our three pieces of jigsaw are particularly interesting and valuable to us because they are the first – and at the moment, only – pieces to be found of what must be a complicated thousand-piece puzzle. All this may seem complicated enough, but in fact it is a gross simplification. There is not one jigsaw puzzle of the Bull Ring but a whole heap of them stacked one on top of the other – there is a medieval puzzle, a Tudor puzzle, a Stuart puzzle, a Georgian puzzle, a Victorian puzzle and so on up to the present day. As we approach the present, the picture on the box generally becomes progressively clearer and more detailed, although not always in a uniform way. From 1731 we have the first good, detailed maps of Birmingham and a wealth of historical documentation. What new

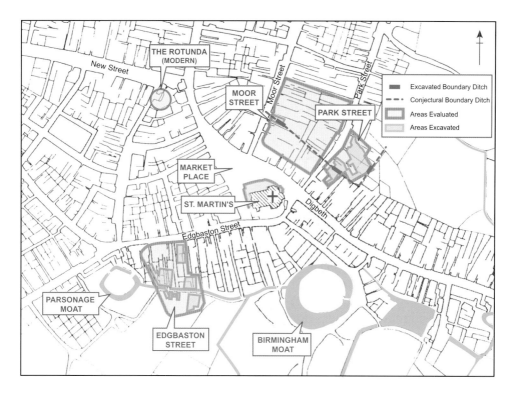

The Bull Ring jigsaw puzzle. The outlines of the puzzle pieces are shown superimposed on a plan of Birmingham in 1751; in the area around the Bull Ring the basic framework of streets and plots had not changed that much since the medieval period. The areas of detailed archaeological excavation are shown in green.

information we learn from painstakingly assembling the pieces of the archaeological jigsaw becomes progressively less and at some point the law of diminishing returns kicks in. But we should never be complacent – the archaeological jigsaw is one of those that, when assembled, is much bigger than the picture on the box. New and unexpected details can be made out, ones that we didn't see on the box. We will see this phenomenon best when we come to consider the excavation of the predominantly 19th-century burials in St. Martin's churchyard. Sometimes, the archaeological jigsaw can make us change our interpretation of the picture in significant ways.

Bearing all these challenges in mind, let's now take a close look at our first puzzle, the medieval puzzle, and our first jigsaw puzzle piece – medieval Edgbaston Street.

Edgbaston Street

Edgbaston Street was probably established early in the life of the market town. It connected to the southwest corner of the triangular market place. To the south of the street a series of characteristic long, thin medieval burgage plots stretched down to the watercourse that once connected the Parsonage Moat with the Birmingham Moat. The general layout of these plots survived into the 18th century, when the first detailed plans of the town were drawn up, and beyond. Being 'watered plots' (i.e. plots provided with a source of running water which could be used for watering animals as well as a variety of light industrial functions) fronting onto one of the main streets of the town near to the market place, these would have been prime properties in the medieval period.

In the early years of the town, the built-up area would have been confined to the stretch of road that led from the market place as far as the Parsonage Moat. The plots nearest to the market place would presumably have been the most desirable and the first to be developed. Beyond the watercourse at the foot of the plots was open countryside, Holme Park, one of the game parks of the de Birmingham family. This open land remained undeveloped countryside right down to the 18th century; the watercourse marked the southern boundary of the built up area of Birmingham for many centuries.

The site of archaeological investigations was located towards the 'out of town' end of Edgbaston Street, adjacent to the former site of the Parsonage Moat. It was a comparatively large 'jigsaw puzzle piece' occupying the whole block between Gloucester Street and Pershore Street, to the east and west, and Upper Dean Street to the south. All three of these streets are late insertions that were absent in medieval times. The block encompassed, towards its southern end, Smithfield Passage, which preserved the line of the former watercourse between the Parsonage Moat and the Birmingham Moat. The land to the south of Smithfield Passage, therefore, would have been undeveloped parkland in the medieval period.

The site was evaluated by means of trial trenching in two stages, the first in 1997 and the second in 1999 when more of the area became available. At the time of the work the majority of the site was used as a car park, and an eight-storey office block, two warehouses and a restaurant were demolished prior to the evaluation.

In all, seven trial trenches were excavated, distributed fairly evenly across the site. The results were mixed. Little of medieval date survived along the Edgbaston Street frontage, where the principal medieval buildings – shops and houses – would have stood, but then this street had been considerably widened in the early 1960s, so many of the plot fronts are actually buried under the road and pavement. Behind the frontage, however, in what would have been the back plots in medieval times, there were several areas with important surviving medieval remains, although often

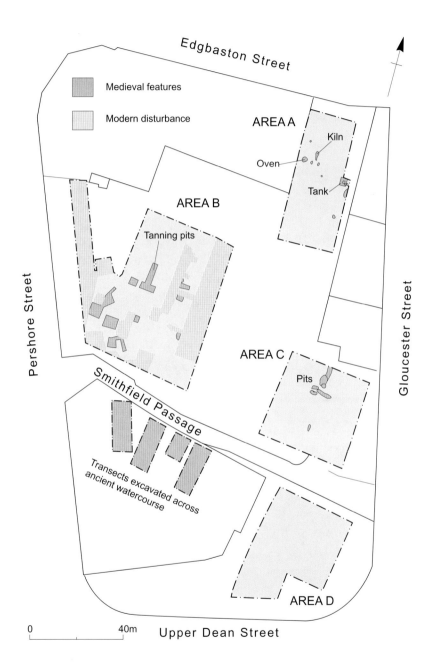

An overall plan of the Edgbaston Street site showing the location of the medieval tanning pits and other features of medieval date.

incomplete and much disturbed by later activity. In terms of the metaphor we have been using, the Edgbaston Street jigsaw puzzle piece had been badly damaged and much of it had been effaced or was illegible. Nevertheless, many interesting and important details survived.

Four areas were selected for further archaeological investigation, one towards the street frontage and the other three exploring areas towards the rear end of the medieval plots, where industrial activity was concentrated. The site is now occupied by the Indoor Market.

The watercourse

One of the earliest surviving features on the site was a stretch of substantial ditch that could be identified as the former watercourse which connected the Parsonage Moat and the Birmingham Moat. The pottery from the soil layers that filled the ditch dated no earlier than the late 13th century but this does not date the watercourse itself, which was probably much older. The pottery was thrown into the ditch along with other domestic rubbish when the watercourse fell largely into disuse; organised refuse collection is only a relatively recent phenomenon and before then much rubbish was disposed of in this way. By modern standards, medieval towns were very dirty, smelly and unpleasant places but they were not entirely unregulated and it was usual for shared resources such as watercourses to be regularly cleared and kept serviceable for the benefit of the population as a whole.

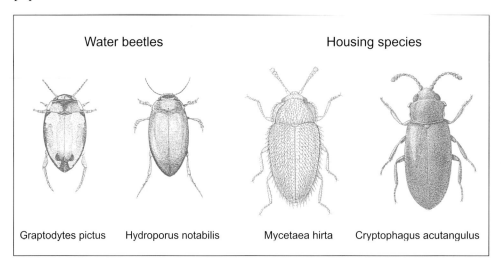

Water beetles		Housing species	
Graptodytes pictus	Hydroporus notabilis	Mycetaea hirta	Cryptophagus acutangulus

Examples of water beetles and 'house fauna' found in the medieval deposits at Edgbaston Street.

The earliest fills of the watercourse were waterlogged and peaty. Such waterlogged soils are very good news for the archaeologist because they preserve the remains of plants and insects which can tell us much about the environment at the time and about the activities that were taking place nearby. Samples are taken from these soils and given to specialists who examine the preserved plant and animal remains in their labs.

Dr David Smith is an archaeologist at the University of Birmingham who specialises in the study of beetles. The beetles remains are extracted from the soil samples by a technique known as 'paraffin flotation' and are then identified under a microscope. Beetles can be very 'picky' about where they live and some feed only on particular species of plant, so they are good indicators of the environment. What David found in the soils from the watercourse were a number of water beetles suggesting the presence of slow flowing or standing water, and strong indications of muddy water. Plant feeding species of leaf beetles and weevils (such as *Prasocuris phellandri* and *Notaris acridulus* – beetles tend to have outlandish names) suggested that the ditch contained reeds, sedges and other aquatic plants. So, if the ditch had once contained free-flowing water, by the time these beetle remains were deposited it was already pretty stagnant.

Other beetle remains told a different story. There were quite large numbers of *Aphodius* dung beetles in the ditch deposits; these species are usually associated with animal dung lying in open grassland. This is interesting because it would tend to support the idea that stock were watered in the back plots, presumably prior to being taken to market. (We know from historical records that trade in livestock was a major function of Birmingham's market.)

Yet other beetle remains confirmed the supposition – first made when we mentioned the pottery – that domestic rubbish was thrown into the ditch, presumably at a later date in the medieval period. There were species associated with wet and rotten rubbish as well as drier human waste – not a pretty picture.

Plant remains from the soils in the ditch present a complementary picture. Dr Marina Ciaraldi and Dr James Grieg, both also of the University of Birmingham, specialise in the study of plant remains from archaeological sites. Marina studies the visible remains of the plants (the so-called 'plant macrofossils') while James specialises in the study of microscopic pollen grains. In the soils from the bottom of the ditch Marina identified the remains of species typical of ditches and watercourses, such as crowfoots, toad-rush, sweet grass and club-rushes. She also found species typical of damp habitats, such as buttercups, bog stitchwort, ragged robin and water pepper. There were also indicators of open or disturbed habitats, such as brambles, common nettle and elder. Willow trees also grew nearby. Further evidence of trees growing near to the ditch was provided by the 'tree-boles' (characteristic shallow, irregular pits caused by tree roots) uncovered by the team of archaeologists led by Cathy Mould.

James' study of the pollen told in part a similar story, but added new elements. Pollen tends to provide a wider picture of the environment than beetles or plant macro fossils; as any hay fever sufferer knows, much pollen is carried by the wind. Pollen of trees and shrubs was relatively infrequent, suggesting no more than some hedgerows and a few alder, oak, hazel and birch trees growing here and there. A few grains of cereal pollen were indicative of cereal cultivation, but more interesting was pollen (from the lowest sample) of broad bean and Cannabaceae, the latter quite possibly hemp. These are typical medieval crops; broad beans were eaten and possibly dried for storage while hemp was widely used for rope making and canvas. Amongst the weeds was cornflower, a characteristic cornfield weed of the medieval period. It need not necessarily have grown nearby but could have come in with straw brought into the town. The majority of the pollen, however, was from a range of plants indicating grassland, such as ribwort plantain and knapweed.

While examining the pollen James made an unexpected find – the egg of a whipworm. This is an internal parasite carried by many animals, especially pigs and humans, and suggests pollution of the watercourse with excrement.

What a lot can be learned from the excavation of just a short stretch of ditch! Most visitors to the archaeological excavation would not have given it a second glance, nor imagine that it was of any real interest, so different is it from the conventional idea of what constitutes an 'archaeological find'. From scientific study of the deposits found in the ditch, however, we can build up a remarkably detailed picture of this corner of the medieval town. It has a decidedly rural feel to it. A watercourse flows through grassland, with a few trees dotted here and there. The watercourse is used to water cattle, whose dung lies on the ground around. The cattle have been brought here to be held, presumably, in a stocking yard prior to butchery or sale in the market. Somewhere in the fields around the town cereal crops are grown as well as broad beans and possibly hemp. The hemp was probably brought into the town to make rope, while straw was brought in for a variety of purposes – for animals, as a floor covering and for thatching.

Counterbalancing this rural 'feel' are reminders that we are on the edge of a busy market town. The watercourse marks the southern edge of plots whose northern end is occupied by buildings fronting onto Edgbaston Street. Over time the watercourse is not well maintained. The water becomes slow moving, reedy or even stagnant. Various sorts of rubbish are dumped in it by the occupants of the houses – rotting waste, broken pottery and even excrement.

The tanning pits

Probably the most important discovery at the Edgbaston Street site was a series of tanning pits. Tanning is the process of converting animal skins into leather by means of soaking them in large pits filled with tannic acid, derived from tree bark, and

Area B of the Edgbaston Street site under excavation, looking west. In the foreground are modern foundations, behind are the medieval tanning pits.

other liquids. Tanning is an unpleasant and smelly process, requiring lots of water, which was often banished to the edges of towns.

The tanning pits were large, rectangular pits measuring up to 5m in length and 0.8m in depth, and were variously wood-lined, clay-lined or simply cut into the subsoil. A number of the pits had stake-holes associated with them – suggesting fencing around them – while one had the remains of a wooden beam at its base. The pits were located towards the back end of the plots, and the majority seemed to be confined to a single plot.

The insect remains from the deposits filling the tanning pits evoke the foul nature of the activities carried out. Large numbers of *Sepsis* flies were recovered; today these species are associated with fluid faecal material and sewage sludges. Also present was a range of water beetles, confirming that the pits had been periodically filled with water. Finally, a number of species were present (although in very small numbers) that are associated with the bark or timber of trees, including various 'bark beetles' and weevils; these are particularly interesting because bark is an ingredient in the tanning process.

The tanning industry in this corner of Birmingham was remarkably long lived. The archaeological excavations showed that the digging of new tanning pits and the reuse of old ones continued right up to the 18th century. Indeed, a map of Birmingham of 1808 by Sheriff shows Welch's Skin Yard occupying part of the site, with the 'Skin Pits' individually marked. However, what is of most interest to us here is the early date at which the tanning industry began here. The pottery – incorporated with ordinary domestic refuse – from some of the pits shows that these particular pits were abandoned and backfilled in the later 13th century, which suggests that tanning started on the site a good few years before that.

The many uses of animals

The tanning pits provide indirect evidence for the exploitation of animals, in particular the hides of cattle. Direct evidence is provided by the bones of the animals themselves. Animal bones are one of the most frequent finds on most archaeological excavations, and the Bull Ring sites were no exception. The bones are mostly found incorporated in dumps of rubbish.

A range of species is represented amongst the animal bones from the medieval levels at Edgbaston Street and the other Bull Ring sites. However, the remains of cattle were everywhere dominant. Cattle can be used for a variety of purposes. Alive, cows provide milk and oxen (castrated males) can be used to pull carts and ploughs. Dead, they provide meat, of course, and hides for leatherworking. Bone and horns are useful materials that can be worked into a variety of artefacts, simple and elaborate. The tough sinews can be used for making thread and string; hooves can even be used to make glue! Because of their multiple uses, the remains of cattle can pass through several hands – the butcher, the tanner, the bone worker, etc (not forgetting the consumer of meat!) – and at each stage the remains will end up amongst the rubbish. Sometimes, from the character of the remains found, the nature of the activity can be inferred.

Generally, hides will be delivered to the tanner or other leatherworker with the horn cores (and sometimes the frontal part of the skull) and feet attached, so where horn cores and foot bones are found together activities associated with the leather trade can be inferred. At Edgbaston Street, the only significant medieval cattle remains comprised horn cores but no foot bones were recovered. Nevertheless, it is reasonable to assume that these largely represent the debris from leatherworking as it was not always the case that the foot bones were left attached to the skins.

The horn cores come from shorthorn beasts (as at the other Bull Ring sites), with cows, oxen and bulls all represented in rough proportion.

The second most important animal represented amongst the bone refuse at Edgbaston Street and the other Bull Ring sites was sheep, which have two main uses of course – wool and meat. Taking the medieval levels at all the Bull Ring sites together for a moment, other animals are much less frequently represented.

Pig, perhaps surprisingly, is very rare, and there are only occasional remains of horse and dog. Historians frequently infer the importance of cattle in the medieval economy of Birmingham, and this is borne out by the animal remains from the Bull Ring sites.

Other activities

The tanning pits aside, the medieval remains over the remainder of the Edgbaston Street site create a less coherent picture – a pit surviving here, a posthole there. However, they do provide a glimpse of the range of activities carried out in the back plots. Just behind where the buildings would have stood on the frontage are three features of interest. The first is a clay-lined oven with a floor surface made of roof tiles; the clay was unburnt, which suggests that the oven may not have been used. The second is a feature which, from its form, can be identified as a kiln. Unfortunately, there were no clues as to what the kiln was used for – grain drying and malting are possibilities – but it and the oven would have been sited well clear of the timber-framed buildings on the frontage to limit the risk of fire.

The third feature in this group is a water cistern or tank. It comprised a large square pit with vertically-cut sides, suggesting it had originally been lined with timber. A smaller square pit was cut into its base. Some of the insects recovered from the fills of the pit seem to bear out the suggestion that it was timber lined as they include two species, the common woodworm and the 'Powder post'

Area A of the Edgbaston Street site was close to the modern street frontage. In the foreground to the left is an 18th-century cellar. The clay-lined oven is amongst the pits just beyond the cellar. On the extreme right, at the edge of the excavation, is the square pit which contained a nearly complete medieval cooking pot.

beetle, both associated with decaying prepared timbers. Also present amongst the insect remains were species of water beetle indicative of slow flowing or still pools of water, suggesting the use of the pit as a water tank. Pollen recovered from the pit supports this suggestion. Amongst the numerous sherds of broken pottery and other rubbish in the pit, which had been dumped in after it ceased to be used as a water tank, was a virtually complete, straight-sided cooking pot – heavily sooted from use – which may not have been a discard but was perhaps deliberately placed in the pit for some unknown reason. This pot and other fragments of pottery in the filling of the pit suggest that the water tank had fallen into disuse in the late 13th century; it may have been constructed decades before then.

It is frustrating that we do not have the evidence to suggest precise functions for this little group of features. This is often the nature of archaeological evidence: it is like watching a group of workmen in the distance – we can see that they are doing something, but what it is we can't quite make out. However one major activity for which there is abundant evidence is the dumping of rubbish. Evidence for it is found in the

A medieval clay-lined oven found close to the street frontage. The floor of the oven is made of roof tiles.

The nearly complete medieval cooking pot, of the late 13th century, found in the square pit. Note the heavy sooting on the pot.

watercourses, in the fillings of disused tanning pits and other pits and ditches; in fact, it is found just about everywhere. This is a good job really, because most of our finds – especially pottery and animal bones – come from such dumps of rubbish. Once again, it is the humble insect which gives us one of the best indications of the nature of this rubbish. All of the soil samples studied by David Smith contained a greater or lesser number of insect species associated with household waste –

mouldering, rotting waste, dry waste and excrement. Indeed, scientists have devised a list of insect species associated with household activities, which have been labelled the 'house fauna,' and all of the core species from this list have been found on the Edgbaston Street site. The remains of the medieval houses which once fronted onto Edgbaston Street may not have survived centuries of building and rebuilding, but there is no doubt that they were there!

Moor Street

The site to the east of Moor Street is the second piece of our archaeological jigsaw puzzle of medieval Birmingham. At first glance it is a big piece, encompassing a large block of land bounded by the Bull Ring to the south, Moor Street. Station to the north, Park Street to the east and Moor Street to the west. Prior to the archaeological investigations in 2000 the buildings occupying the block – including a 1960s multi-story office block and car park and a pub, The Ship Ashore – were demolished. Trial trenches were excavated over much of the site to test for the survival of archaeological deposits close to the street frontage, across historic boundaries and within back plot areas. Unfortunately, it soon became clear that the building activity in the 20th century had scoured away all earlier remains down to the level of the sandstone bedrock across most of the site. In only one small area, around the concrete piles that had supported the former Ship Ashore pub on Moor Street, did reasonably well preserved remains of the medieval period survive, and it was here that the archaeological excavation took place. The only other significant survival was a sandstone-lined medieval well situated close to the Bull Ring frontage.

Thus the Moor Street jigsaw puzzle piece has been largely erased, but nevertheless what did survive shed considerable light on life in medieval Birmingham.

The boundary ditch

Once again, as at Edgbaston Street, a rich story can be wrung from a feature as unprepossessing as a boundary ditch, if it is analysed carefully. The earliest archaeological feature on the site was a massive ditch 4.4m wide and 1.65m deep. The ditch ran back from Moor Street on a line roughly parallel with the curving Bull Ring frontage, and would have formed the rear boundary to plots fronting onto the market place before Moor Street was laid out. We will come across a ditch on a similar alignment when we come to discuss the results of the Park Street excavations, so this was clearly a major boundary feature; as well as acting as a watercourse it served as the boundary between one of the lord's game parks, Little (or Over) Park, and the town. Therefore, fronting directly onto the market place and

The excavation at Moor Street, looking east. Underneath the concrete foundation piles for the 'Ship Ashore' pub can be seen the massive medieval boundary ditch.

provided with a running water supply behind, these plots, like the ones on Edgbaston Street, were amongst the best in the medieval town and, as such, would have been developed relatively early in the life of the town. So, from what was found in the ditch how much can we infer of what was going on nearby?

The story of the ditch is itself quite complicated, as can be seen from the cross-section through the fills within the ditch. Early in its history the ditch was recut along its original alignment but to a somewhat narrower width (3.80m); such thorough clearing

A stone-lined medieval well uncovered close to the Bull Ring frontage.

out of the ditch would have been necessary from time to time. Then the ditch would start to silt up again, and – as at Edgbaston Street – people would from time to time dump their rubbish in it. Eventually, by the late 13th century, the ditch had fallen

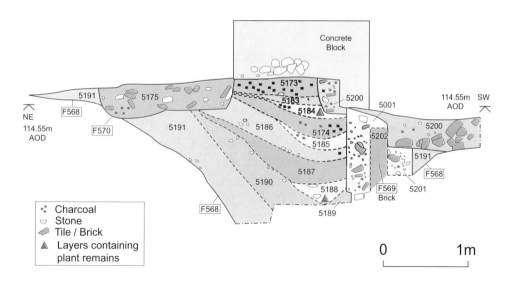

A cross-section through the boundary ditch on the Moor Street site. Each soil layer filling the ditch is given a unique number so that finds and environmental samples can be accurately located. The layers from which plant remains were recovered are indicated.

into disuse and as far as it survived (the top of the ditch had been scoured away by 20th-century building) had completely filled up.

Two samples from the ditch contained well-preserved plant remains, which were studied in detail by Marina Ciaraldi. The first of these samples came from a deposit near to the bottom of the recut ditch, and probably dates to the early 13th century. This sample contained, almost exclusively, the remains of plants associated with disturbed ground, such as the common nettle and elder. Plants associated with wet environments, such as sedges and rushes, were also present, and presumably represent plants growing along the edge of the water-filled ditch. All of this is consistent with the nearby presence of parkland and a relatively low level of human activity.

The second sample, from much higher up in the deposits filling the ditch and probably dating to the late 13th century, contained a much more diversified range of plants. There were many weeds and grassland plants and plants of wet and disturbed ground. Most interestingly the sample also contained a substantial group of cereals. In fact it is the largest group of cereal remains recovered in the whole of the excavations, and provides us with a picture of some of the crops grown in the fields around medieval Birmingham. Bread/club wheat, barley, oat and rye are all present. Several of the grains had germinated, suggesting that they might have been used for malting in beer-making or that they had been spoilt during storage and were therefore used for fodder.

To Marina, the presence of grassland species together with the large number of oat grains and other germinated cereals, strongly indicated that the whole collection of plant remains probably represented charred fodder. Even the numerous weeds in the collection – plants such as stinking chamomile and corn marigold which are often found as weeds in cornfields – might represent the waste of crop processing used as fodder. So here, again, is evidence for the back plots being used for the keeping of animals.

James Greig's study of a sample of microscopic pollen from the ditch provides a complementary picture to that derived from the study of the larger plant 'macrofossils'. Perhaps the most striking aspect of the pollen sample was that just under half of it was tree pollen, mainly alder, hazel and oak, with a little birch, lime and holly. There must have been quite dense woodland nearby, or perhaps the pollen came into the town with woodland products such as firewood, brushwood or tanning bark. James also found grassland, wetland and crop species represented, mirroring Marina's findings. Amongst the crops, James spotted flax which, in the medieval period was used for its fibres and its seeds, which could be used for linseed oil or eaten. Finally, he spotted the eggs of intestinal parasites, indicating some contamination of the ditch with sewage.

The ditch, as we have seen, fell into disuse in the late 13th century and became filled up with rubbish. The pottery evidence suggests that the ditch was not backfilled in one go, but that this was a more gradual process. The most likely context for the disuse of the ditch and its filling up is the insertion of Moor Street across the line of the ditch. So, indirectly, this gives us a date for the laying out of this street.

Pits and industry

After the ditch had fallen into disuse and had become filled up, a series of pits were dug into it and adjacent to it. Whatever the original purpose of the pits they were ultimately used for the disposal of rubbish (one contained bones from a small pony). The rubbish itself suggests a mixture of industrial and domestic activities. One pit of interest contained a large quantity of charcoal and all the sherds of pottery found in it were badly burnt – did this pit contain debris cleared from a house fire? House fires were rather common in medieval towns, but there is a documentary reference to a 'great fire' in Birmingham around 1300 and the date of the pottery fits.

Remains found in the fills of the ditch and the pits provide our first hint of the metalworking industries for which Birmingham was to become so famous. A fragment of a crucible was found, together with hammerscale, which is the debris resulting from the hammering of hot iron. Fragments of coal were also frequently found, which is likely to be the fuel used for the industrial processes.

In general, what we seem to be seeing at Moor Street is an intensification of activity, beginning perhaps in the late 12th century and continuing through to the 14th century, with domestic, agricultural and industrial activities all represented. Almost all evidence of later activity had been scoured away by 20th-century buildings. Today the site is buried under Selfridges.

Park Street

The Park Street site is the third and final piece of the medieval Bull Ring jigsaw puzzle; it was also the last to be investigated, from February to July 2001. The site lay to the east of Park Street and to the south of Moor Street Station. It is now occupied by a multi-storey car park serving the new Bullring shopping centre.

The archaeological investigations proceeded in the usual manner. Following a desk-top assessment of the archaeological potential of the site, four trial trenches were dug into accessible areas of the site. The results were promising, with a sequence of remains surviving extensively across the site dating from the 12th or 13th centuries (at around 1m below the modern ground surface) onwards. For more detailed investigation, three larger areas, labelled A, B and C, were opened in sequence, in order to fit round the contractors' demolition works and avoid areas obliterated by 19th- and 20th-century cellaring and other activity. The result was a

The Park Street excavations in progress, 2001.

jigsaw puzzle piece of rather complicated and irregular shape – fragmentary and damaged as ever – but nevertheless one revealing a substantial chunk of the medieval townscape.

Roads, boundaries and town planning

To understand the site, it is important to appreciate how the jigsaw puzzle piece fits into the overall plan of medieval Birmingham. Across the southwestern end of the site, at right angles to Park Street, ran a massive ditch, surviving to a width of 7m and to a depth of at least 2m. This is almost certainly a continuation of the major boundary ditch excavated on the Moor Street site, and defined the rear boundary of burgage plots fronting onto the market place and the upper end of Digbeth. At Park Street, however, the main area of the archaeological site did not lie 'inside' this boundary – i.e. within the plots fronting onto the market place and upper Digbeth – but 'outside' the boundary in land which would, in the earliest years of the market town, have lain within one of the lord of the manor's hunting parks, Little (or Over) Park.

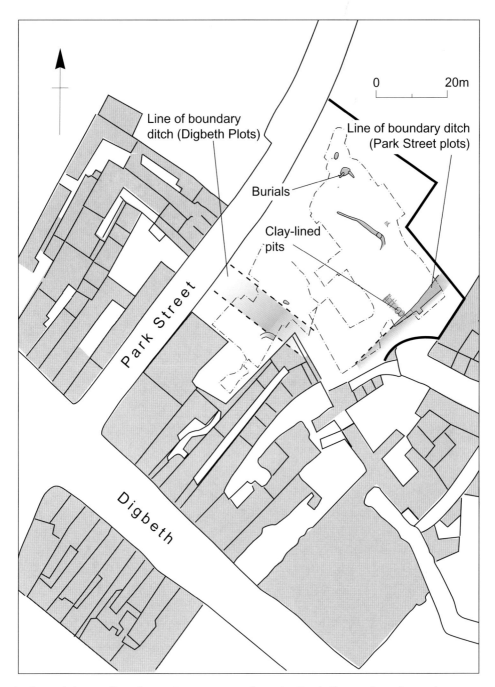

A plan of the medieval remains uncovered on the Park Street site, shown in relationship to the street and plot layout in the early 20th century.

*A section cut through the large medieval boundary ditch which ran across the
Park Street site. The rods are 2m in length.*

Only when Park Street (or Little Park Street as it was occasionally called) was
inserted across Little Park would the area of the excavations have become part of
the town, with plots laid out fronting onto Park Street. At this point, the old
boundary ditch would have become redundant both as an important boundary
feature and as a watercourse (the new road blocking the flow). Perhaps, as may also
have been the case for the Moor Street section of the ditch, it was replaced by a
culverted watercourse or drain following a similar line (something would need to be
done to control the water), but if so no trace of this has survived. In any case, the
ditch became filled up with rubbish. What is interesting is that the pottery found
amongst the rubbish suggests that the ditch was filled in slightly later than the Moor
Street section to the west, perhaps in the early 14th rather than the late 13th century.
From this we might infer that Park Street was laid out later than Moor Street, which
is perfectly logical if Moor Street and Park Street are seen as progressive
encroachments onto the lord of the manor's park.

The new plots laid out fronting onto Park Street were bounded along their back
ends by a new ditch, dug running parallel to Park Street and perpendicular to the
old boundary ditch. Only one edge of this new boundary ditch, which had been

cleared out or 'recut' early in its history, lay within the area of the excavations, for the simple reason that its line still formed the boundary to the building plot down to the present day and was followed by the line of a 19th-century wall. Such remarkable continuity of property boundaries down the centuries was one of the major findings of the Bull Ring excavations. This does not mean that the ditch survived as a visible feature for very long – the few sherds of pottery recovered from it indicate that it was infilled in the 14th century (providing evidence that Park Street must have been laid out before this) – but that its course became 'fossilised' as a property boundary. The same phenomenon can be seen in the case of the old boundary ditch, the line of which was respected in the layout of 19th-century buildings.

The successive laying out of Moor Street and then Park Street, together with the digging of a ditch to define the end of the properties fronting onto the latter, are an example of medieval town planning. Here we are witnessing the deliberate expansion of Birmingham, probably somewhere in the 13th century. As the new streets and building plots were carved out of one of the lord of the manor's parks, we can be sure that the de Birmingham family was involved in the project, which was no doubt principally aimed at generating yet more lucrative rents for the lord.

Pottery production

As we have already seen, boundary ditches – and even more so the rubbish found in them – can tells us a lot about what was going on around them. Stephanie Rátkai, the specialist who studied the pottery from the Bull Ring excavations, noticed several unusual things about a group of more than 300 sherds of pottery recovered from the soil filling the old boundary ditch. The pottery was of a type called 'Deritend ware', produced predominantly in the 13th century. Deritend ware was first described in the 1950s, when 'wasters' (the mis-fired and distorted sherds that occur when a pottery firing goes wrong) were found during excavations on Deritend High Street. The presence of wasters shows that pottery production took place locally, although the pottery kilns themselves have not been found. Since the 1950s, further Deritend ware wasters have been found elsewhere in Deritend – for example in pits at the Old Crown in 1994 and at Hartwell's Garage in Digbeth in 2000 – indicating pottery production on a substantial scale. The most characteristic type of vessels produced in Deritend ware were jugs in a red fabric decorated with a white slip, but cooking pots were also produced and, in smaller numbers, bowls, pipkins and dripping trays.

Of the large group of sherds found in the Park Street ditch, a large proportion had 'patchy' surface colouration, indicating poor control over the firing conditions; many also had cracked surfaces, and chipping or flaking of the rim of the pot was

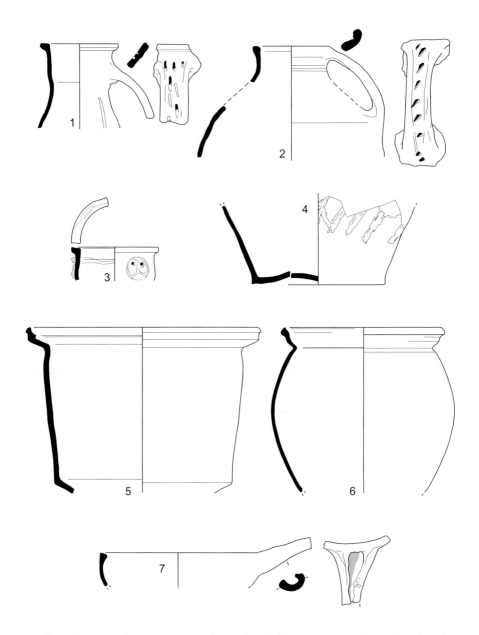

Examples of Deritend ware pottery from the Bull Ring excavations. Deritend ware was produced at several sites in Birmingham, including Park Street, from the 13th to the early 14th century. 1 & 2 – Jugs; 3 – Jug with face mask; 4- Jug base broken ('wastered') during firing; 5 & 6 – Cooking pots; 7 – Pipkin.

common. Virtually all the pot sherds had no trace of sooting on them, which, in the case of cooking pots, suggests they might not have been used. Taken together, the evidence points very strongly to the group of sherds being waste from pottery production. A clincher was the finding, elsewhere in the ditch, of part of a fire-bar (a clay bar used to support pots stacked in a kiln).

So pottery production was taking place not just in Deritend but in the heart of medieval Birmingham on the Park Street site; there was even the odd possible waster on the Moor Street site also. Medieval Birmingham's pottery industry may have been very extensive; the discovery of its existence is entirely a consequence of archaeological investigations – there is not a single documentary reference to potters in the historical record, though many other trades are mentioned. However, it is perhaps a good thing that we do not have a record of the language used when a pottery firing went wrong!

Examples of decoration on Deritend ware jugs. 1 – White slip and applied scale decoration; 2 – Roller-stamped white slip decoration; 3 – White chevron decoration; 4 – Brushed white slip bands; 5 – Horizontal combing on shoulder above white slip lattice.

When Stephanie plotted out the distribution of wasters, mis-fires, fire-bars and the like, it was clear that nearly all the material came from the old boundary ditch and adjacent layers at the southwestern end of the site. This suggested that the pottery kilns themselves were located in the early burgage plots fronting onto the market place/Digbeth rather than the later plots fronting onto Park Street. This is curious because pottery production is a dirty, smoky business, carrying a high fire risk; it was usually banished to the edge of towns, like tanning which is unpleasant in other ways. However, in Birmingham we have evidence of both pottery production and tanning (at the Edgbaston Street site) close to the town centre, which helps us to form a picture of what medieval Birmingham was like.

Textiles and leather working

We have already seen how the remains of plants and insects from ditches and pits are a treasure house of information about the environment of a site and the activities which went on at and around it. The general picture gained from analysis of the remains at Edgbaston Street and Moor Street was repeated at Park Street – around the site was a mixture of woodland, grassland and crop fields, the ditches themselves were originally water filled but soon became a focus for the dumping of all kinds of rubbish. Here, we will just pick out one or two points of interest.

Amongst the plant remains recovered were those of hemp and flax. It is likely that hemp and flax were being processed on the site for their fibres. Hemp was used to make ropes and canvas while flax is used to make linen.

A number of apparently clay-lined pits or tanks situated adjacent to the 'new' boundary ditch to the rear of the Park Street plots are likely to have held water and may have been used for a variety of industrial purposes, including textile processing, dyeing, horn working, leather working and smithing. However, in most cases the absence of clear evidence for the function of these pits or tanks leaves their use uncertain. Some support for leather working having taken place at Park Street is provided by the animal bones found, which are dominated by cattle horn cores and foot elements, a characteristic 'signature' of leather working.

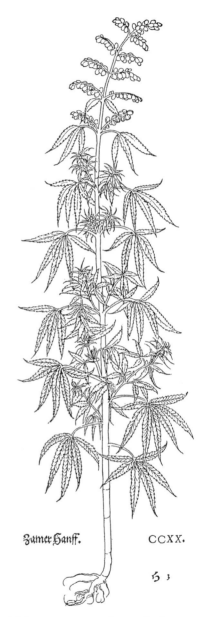

Zamer Hanff.   CCXX.

ß ʒ

A 16th-century woodcut of a hemp plant. Hemp seeds were found at the Park Street excavations, where hemp may have been processed to make ropes and canvas.

Ironworking

Although there were hints at Moor Street, it is at Park Street that we get the first substantial evidence of metalworking on the Bull Ring sites. The manufacture of metal items was to become the backbone of Birmingham's growth and prosperity in later centuries, a story we shall pursue in Chapter 5, so archaeological evidence of its medieval origins is of great interest – from small acorns do mighty oaks grow.

As with so much else on the Bull Ring excavations, the evidence of medieval metalworking is not to be found in intact structures – no smithing hearths survived, for example – but amongst the 'rubbish' found in ditches, pits and general 'occupation layers'. The study of 'metalworking debris' is one of the many specialist scientific skills, alongside the study of plant remains, insects, animal bone and pottery, necessary for the interpretation of archaeological sites. The metalworking debris from Park Street was studied by Matthew Nicholas. The majority of his work focussed on analysing crucibles and their contents of the 17th and 18th centuries, with some fascinating results which we will look at in Chapter 6, but for the medieval period the evidence consisted almost exclusively of slag, and most of it 'undiagnostic slag' at that. This slag was found distributed over more or less the whole site, suggesting that metalworking was an activity carried out extensively to the rear of Park Street.

Slag is the waste from the hot working of metals. When a craftsman makes a metal item there will be two products, the item itself and the debris from its production. Ninety-nine times out of a hundred (or probably worse), all the archaeologist will find is the debris – the finished item is taken away to be sold in a shop or a market. Unlike pottery, if the manufacturing process goes wrong the result (a 'waster') will not be thrown away but will be collected up for a second attempt – metal is recyclable and even finished items are frequently recycled, often to considerable profit. The slag, however, is just left lying around or cleared away into pits and ditches, hopefully for an archaeologist to find centuries later. It is not the sort of thing that you will generally find in a museum case, but it is invaluable evidence nonetheless.

Basically, slag comes in two forms, 'smelting slag' (the residue from the extraction of the metal from its ore), and 'smithing slag' (the residue from making the extracted metal into useful items). There was no indication at Park Street that smelting had taken place, all the slag was probably smithing slag. This is not too surprising, although there is not a great deal of evidence for this period, smelting was probably carried out by itinerant 'bloomsmiths' exploiting the ironstone outcrops around Dudley, Walsall and Wednesbury (the beginning of a long and fruitful relationship between the resources of the Black Country and the market of Birmingham). The product would have been delivered to the Park Street smiths in the form of 'bar iron' for smithing, a specialised activity producing higher value and lighter weight commodities that would have tended to congregate close to market and urban centres.

What the Park Street smiths made we can only guess (the humble but crucially important nail – imagine life without it – was no doubt on the menu and was found in some quantity in medieval layers). Nor, indeed, can we be certain that all the slag is the result of iron working. Most of the slag from the medieval layers is 'undiagnostic', as we noted, but as the small quantity (mostly later) that is diagnostic does indicate ironworking, it is a reasonable guess. Some of the medieval slag from Park Street is categorised as 'hearth bottom'. This comprises pieces of slag with a characteristic bowl shape, which indicates that they accumulated at the bottom of the smithing hearth. Much of the 'hearth bottom' at Park Street contained lumps of coal, which is direct evidence for the fuel used by the smiths. This is important because coal is a fuel that has to be mined and is only found in certain places. Again, our best bet is the exposed coalfield of the Black Country, where there are several documented medieval workings around Dudley, Wednesbury and Halesowen – another early indication of the Birmingham-Black Country link that was to become so important later on.

Ironworking, like pottery manufacture, is a high-temperature industry carrying a serious fire risk. It is interesting, therefore, that a common find amongst the rubbish – along with the pot sherds, animal bones and slag – was pieces of roof tile. Buildings with tiled roofs are considerably less of a fire risk than those with thatched roofs, and this may explain the apparent widespread use of tile in this part of Birmingham in the medieval period.

A murder mystery?

Every now and then archaeological excavations turn up something very unexpected. This was the case on the Park Street excavations. In the northeast corner of the site, close to the street frontage, two well-preserved human skeletons were found. The bodies had been buried in earth-cut graves, laid out on their backs with the arms folded across the stomach. There were no obvious signs of haste in the burials.

While human burials are not that uncommon on archaeological excavations, from the medieval period onwards we expect to find them in formal burial grounds, usually churchyards. When we find them under the floor or in the backyard we usually expect foul play. Furthermore, the Christian practice is to bury the body aligned east-west, with the head to the east. While, one of the corpses was laid out this way, the other was laid out on a north-south alignment with the head to the north. Very fishy.

Who were these two? We can't discover their identities, of course, but careful scientific study of their skeletons can tell us quite a lot about them. The study was carried out by Rachel Ives of the University of Birmingham. Rachel used

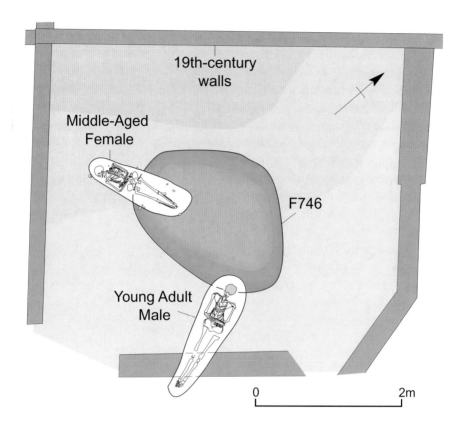

19th-century
walls

Middle-Aged
Female

F746

Young Adult
Male

0   2m

The two mysterious burials close to the Park Street frontage.

measurements on the pelvis and the skull to determine the sex of the skeletons, and one turned out to be a probable female and the other a probable male (human bodies are very variable so you can rarely be absolutely sure of the sex of a skeleton). Growth changes of the skull, age-related degeneration of bone and tooth wear were the methods Rachel used to assess the age at death of the skeletons. The female turned out to be middle aged and the male a young adult, probably 18-22 years old.

The young man's short life seems to have been quite tough. Defects of the spine indicated that he had strained his back, perhaps through spending much of his time engaged in heavy manual labour. He had injured his shin at some time also, which had become inflamed and had not healed properly, perhaps because of a diet poor in the vitamin C necessary for proper healing. A poor diet was also indicated by his teeth, which were very decayed; most of his teeth were affected by caries and the crowns of several had been destroyed by severe caries. His dental enamel also displayed lots of defects, the cause of which is most likely to be illness or nutritional inadequacy during childhood. There were, however, no clues as to the cause of death.

The middle-aged woman seems to have enjoyed better health, prior to whatever it was that caused her death. Unlike the young man, her teeth were extensively worn, with large amounts of dentine exposed, but this was just a reflection of the age difference between the two and the nature of the woman's diet, which must have included quite a lot of 'gritty' food; only two of her teeth were affected by caries. Again, there was no clue as to the cause of death.

Why were these two bodies buried where they were, outside of any known cemetery? There are several possibilities, an obvious one being murder and clandestine burial. The unusual orientation of one of the burials and the absence of shroud pins suggest these were not formal burials. Alternatively, it is not uncommon to deny Christian burial in a churchyard to those who have transgressed Christian morals in some way – adulterers, heretics, suicides and murderers.

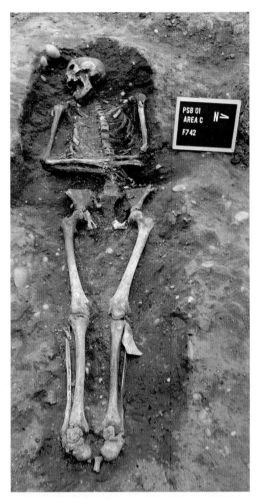

Grave of middle-aged female, probably medieval in date, found on the Park Street site.

However, the date of the burials is not absolutely certain. The pottery specialist, Stephanie Rátkai, looked at the question closely. The two graves were cut into layers and a filled-in pit containing pottery that suggested that the earliest date possible for the digging of the graves was the second half of the 13th century. The pottery found in the soil infilling the graves (which was, of course, just bits of broken pottery lying around and accidentally incorporated in the grave filling) also indicated a medieval date, as did the pottery from the layers immediately overlying the graves. However, despite the predominance of medieval pottery there were one or two sherds of 17th-century blackwares and yellow wares in the soils associated with the burials. Normally we would dismiss the odd sherd of later pottery as 'intrusive' but it is just possible that they are not and that the burials were, indeed, made in the 17th century. This does not make them any less mysterious, but it does provide a possible historical context for the burials. Stephanie speculated that the burials might be associated with the Civil War 'Battle of Birmingham'.

The townspeople of Birmingham, who had already something of a non-conformist reputation, held to the Parliamentarian cause. It was also alleged that they manufactured swords to supply the Parliamentary army. On Easter Monday 1643 Prince Rupert, entered the town with a force of around 2,000 men to teach them a lesson. Birmingham had no defences and a few earth barricades were easily circumvented. Prince Rupert's men ransacked and burnt part of the town. According to a Parliamentary pamphlet, with an obvious propaganda point to make, 'They ran into every house cursing and damning and threatening and terrifying the poore Women most terribly, setting naked Swords and Pistols to their breasts, they fell to plundering all the Town before them...'.

The moſt Illuſtrious and High borne PRINCE RUPERT, PRINCE ELECTOR. Second Son to FREDERICK KING of BOHEMIA, GENERALL of the HORSE of Hs MAJESTIES ARMY, KNIGHT of the Noble Order of the GARTER.

*A woodcut of Prince Rupert. It forms the frontispiece to **Burning Love**, a Parliamentarian account of the Battle of Birmingham printed in 1643.*

But we are getting ahead of ourselves, before leaving medieval Birmingham, we want to attempt to use the new evidence from archaeology, in tandem with historical evidence, to paint a portrait of the medieval town. This is the subject of the next chapter.

Chapter 4

A Portrait of Medieval Birmingham

Steve Litherland with Simon Buteux

Having surveyed the archaeological evidence, it is time to try and get a feel for what the medieval town was actually like and how it changed over the years since the market was founded. We shall do this first through the eyes of a fictional character – an old medieval knight – who has returned to Birmingham after many years of absence. The knight follows the same route into the town up Digbeth as a later real visitor, the travelling scholar John Leland, who visited the town and recorded his impressions of it in 1538.

A knight's tale

The date is 1230 and a tired old knight is returning to Dudley Castle – where he had once done his military training many years previously – to pay homage to his lord. Stopping to let his horse drink from one of the meandering channels of the River Rea he turns to survey the scene around him, lit by the dying rays of an autumnal

An old knight returns to Birmingham in 1230.

Although this view of Birmingham from the southwest dates from 1731, five-hundred years later than the visit of the fictional knight, the character of the old part of Birmingham had not changed that much. The knight enters Birmingham through Deritend, shown on the extreme right, crosses the River Rea and climbs up Digbeth, lined with houses and workshops, to the market place and St. Martin's Church on the extreme left. He leaves the town skirting Holme Park, shown in the foreground.

sun. What strikes him most is the extent to which everything has changed from when he had last taken this route on his way to danger and adventure in Normandy and the Holy Land. For the past 20 miles he had travelled through what was once largely woodland, heath and rough pasture but now sported enclosures, squatter settlements and moated homesteads. There on the hill behind him, Bordesley – once a backwater – is even at this late hour busy with people harvesting the last of the corn. Down by the river another group is absorbed in the mowing of hay from the meadows. Even in Deritend, which in living memory was merely a fording point over the Rea dotted with a few houses, smoke is beginning to rise from many fires lit to take the bite off the cool evening air. The acrid smoke hangs in wisps above the gently flowing river and mingles with odours carried down from the town above. The old knight's nose picks out the distinct and sickly smell of tanning hides, which is mixed with a sweeter one of fodder and manure from cattle corralled in pens, waiting to become food and jerkins or shoes or saddles.

Picking his way across the Rea by means of a raised causeway he enters Birmingham proper, passing the closed toll booth on the far bank of the river, the wet clay of the valley floor clinging to his horse's shoes. Then the ground slowly begins to rise, the gradient getting progressively steeper, but as his horse labours up the slope past the odd open-fronted smithy, or drying rack for hides, he realises that

Medieval blacksmiths at work, mid-14th century. From the 13th century onwards there is evidence of ironworking at both the Park Street and Moor Street sites.

his luck is in, and that he will have no trouble getting a hot meal and bed to spend the night in one of the dense cluster of buildings surrounding the market place. For while the manor house is still there to his left, surrounded by the dark flat water of the moat, and his soldier's eye instinctively notices the sharp silhouette of the church against the darkening sky, the rest of the settlement has changed out of all recognition. This is now a proper market town boasting the usual array of choices and temptations for the unwary traveller. What a difference from his father's day when the market place had first been set out, and men with measuring poles had divided up the building plots around its edges, while a gang of masons began to lay the first stones of the church in the market place. Now St. Martin's church already seems too small to cater for such a rapidly expanding population. Why, he says to himself, this place has really started to 'make it', in every sense of the expression.

Enquiring after the whereabouts of a decent hostelry from the driver of a heavily-loaded cart, lumbering up the hill towards a large hayrick beside the cattle pens, he dismounts and, with the church behind him, begins to pick his way through the stalls that are being set up for the market tomorrow. He only pauses to wash away some of the dust from the road with fresh water drawn from one of the public stone-lined wells at this end of the market. Stopping at last in front of a large timber-framed inn he beckons to an ostler who takes his horse round to the back for a rub down and to drink from the stream running along the backplot of the house. Inside, he settles for the 'special' of Welsh beef and vegetable stew and orders a flagon of ale that is served in an orange-glazed flagon with white painted slip patterning, the likes of which he has not seen before. He is assured by the hostess that it is a new design made by the pottery nearby. He resolves to buy one in the market tomorrow as a gift before setting out for Dudley, together with a new pair of hose as he will need to look smart for his appointment with his lord. Several flagons later, and after relating many (only slightly embroidered) tales of his exploits in the Holy Land to a rowdy group of potters and smiths, he confesses to his new companions that at his time of life he should really think about settling down. They tell him that for a price a freeman can buy the privileges of a burgess from the lord of Birmingham and set himself up comfortably in the booming town. Thoughtful, he turns in for the night, first making sure that his horse is properly fed and watered and content.

The next day he awakes (with only a slightly sore head) to the noise of a market already going about its business. The butchers, fishmongers, bakers and shoemakers are rather too loudly proclaiming the quality and value of their wares and, after picking up the pottery and hose for a good price, he makes his way towards Dudley down the road at the bottom of the market, leading off to Edgbaston to his west. As he leaves the town he looks back for a moment and his eye passes over yet more watered plots on this side of the market, where hunched figures are busy at work digging a new tanning pit, and over the manor house and moat overlooking rolling meadow and parkland, where a deer darts out of the shade of the trees and into the low morning sunlight. Yes, he thinks to himself, he might discuss his future options with his lord in Dudley; there were clearly opportunities in Birmingham for a man with a bit of enterprise and here would be a good place to begin a new chapter in his life.

The evolving town

The knight is pure fiction, of course, but the description of the Birmingham he visits in the early 13th century is based largely on the archaeological

A medieval leather merchant displays his wares.

45

evidence we surveyed in the previous chapter, together with a study of the topography of the town and the few scraps of historical evidence that have survived. Like the knight we will now look back and review the evidence for the development of medieval Birmingham in a more sober fashion.

The medieval town plan

The heart of medieval Birmingham was the triangular market place (the name 'Bull Ring' is of much later origin) with St. Martin's church within it. Here, important roads converged at the three corners of the triangle – Digbeth on the southeast corner, High Town (essentially a continuation of Digbeth) on the north corner and Edgbaston Street on the southwest corner. The prime development sites were around the market place itself and along the streets approaching it, through

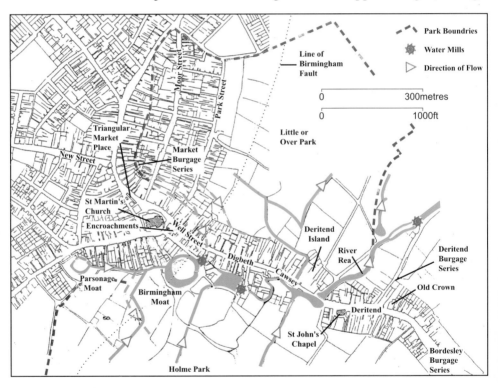

Birmingham's ancient water system shown in relationship to the plan of the town in 1751. Note how the system of streams and ditches provides a water supply to most of the plots surrounding the market place and down Digbeth as far as the River Rea. Most of Birmingham's industry, such as smithing and tanning, was concentrated here.

which most of the traffic would pass. Space on the frontages of the market and the approaching streets was most at a premium, and the need was to squeeze as many properties as possible into these prime locations. This explains the shape of the typical medieval building plot (or 'burgage plot' as it is known), not just in Birmingham but in all medieval towns. It is long and thin, laid out at right angles to the market or street frontage. The main building, perhaps a shop and/or residence, occupies the precious location on the frontage, while a long strip of land – the back plot – stretches out behind it. The back plot could be used for a variety of purposes – market gardening, keeping animals, industrial activities of various kinds and rubbish disposal. As we have seen, nearly all of the archaeological evidence uncovered in the Bull Ring excavations relates to this sort of 'back plot' activity.

The basic plan of medieval Birmingham is mainly inferred from 18th- and 19th-century maps and surveys for the simple reason that earlier maps with sufficient detail do not exist. It is a fortunate fact that once property boundaries are established they often remain stable for centuries. Buildings may come and go, but property boundaries tend to remain substantially unaltered. After all, the logic of the burgage plot – maximising use of expensive frontage locations – is not restricted to the medieval period. Thus it is possible with careful study to discern in 18th- and 19th-century maps the pattern of Birmingham's medieval streets and burgage plots with reasonable confidence.

It was only when a new logic prevailed – like that of the railway train in the 1840s, or the motor car and the shopping centre in the 1960s and 70s – that the medieval pattern became substantially obscured for much of Birmingham city centre. Unfortunately, even in those parts of the city not directly affected by major developments such as railway lines and stations, the Inner Ring Road or the 1960s Bull Ring Centre, road widening to accommodate the motor vehicle has often resulted in the loss of medieval street frontages, which is one reason why the survival of archaeological remains is so often confined to the back plots.

The importance of water

Revealing the importance of watered plots in medieval Birmingham is one of the major findings of the Bull Ring excavations. We have seen how a prime development plot was one that fronted on to the market place or one of the major streets approaching it. But such a plot was doubly valuable if it also had a good supply of water. This could be achieved by arranging things such that while the front end of the plot faced onto the market or street, the back end terminated in a watercourse. These so-called 'watered plots' would be in particular demand, and indeed are a frequent feature of early market towns. Livestock could be grazed and watered close to the market – such plots would be particularly valuable to the town's butchers – while industries such as hide tanning, dyeing and hemp or flax retting all demand a good supply of water.

However, in a different way Birmingham suffered from an excess of water because the wide and flat valley bottom of the River Rea was regularly prone to flooding. Even as late as 1852 flooding caused the south-eastern quarter of Birmingham to be covered by a sheet of water several feet deep and a quarter of a mile wide along the whole length of the river. In the medieval period, this

Reconstruction drawing of an iron cauldron from Edgbaston Street.

was where the lord's meadows lay in two large parks – an important resource as a supply of feed for cattle, but significantly in 1232 the onerous obligation of haymaking was one that 16 tenants negotiated their way out of in exchange for cash payments; in the burgeoning town they had better ways to spend their time and could afford to buy their freedom. On the other hand, the higher ground to the north of the Birmingham fault was blessed with lighter, warmer, sandier soils that were far easier to dig and use. Therefore, we have the topographical basis for a real split between the types of settlement and activity carried out in the low and high town in later periods, and the dividing line between where buildings would have been at risk of flooding and where they were not is likely to have been an important one.

The development of the town

As we saw in Chapter 1, no archaeological evidence for settlement earlier than the 12th century was found in any of the excavations around the Bull Ring (excluding slight traces of much earlier prehistoric and Roman activity). So we will start our review of the evidence for the development of medieval Birmingham with the earliest remains found during the excavations. These were the large boundary ditch found behind the plots fronting the northeastern side of the market place in the Moor Street and Park Street excavations, and pottery from the Edgbaston Street site.

The water-filled ditch ran on a line roughly parallel with the curving frontage of the market place. It may have been a natural feature following the sinuous line of a small depression cut by a stream flowing at right angles to the sandstone ridge here. Alternatively, it may have been deliberately dug to follow the line of a pre-existing boundary, say to a field, or specifically to mark the edge of Little (or Over) Park. Students of the medieval townscape look for evidence of regularity and planning, and where this does not happen look for reasons why. These are often to do with the adaptation of an idealised scheme to an awkward site.

An instance of this occurs in Birmingham where the group of burgage plots facing the northeastern side of the market place become noticeably shorter the further down the hill you go because their back ends were defined by the ditch. This implies that the ditch and the burgage plots were not laid out at the same time but that the plots had to squeeze up against the pre-existing ditch. This was probably because, fronting directly onto the market place and provided with a running water supply behind, these plots were amongst the best in the medieval town and the provision of running water was more important at this time than the setting out of a completely regular plot pattern. This ditch forming the rear boundary to the plots fronting onto the northeastern side of the market, and picked up in both the Moor Street and Park Street excavations, has been identified by one scholar, George Demidowicz, as the 'Hersum Ditch', a name which appears in a series of deeds relating to properties on Moor Street dating from 1341 to 1681. However, the fact that by the 14th century this ditch had been filled in, as the Moor Street and Park Street excavations show, must make this identification questionable.

The archaeological evidence also indicates that the plots towards the western end of Edgbaston Street were laid out as watered plots in the 12th century, with the watercourse between the two moats forming the southern boundary of the plots. Pollen and seeds show us that Birmingham lay in a well-wooded landscape typical of the northern part of Warwickshire, often called the Arden. The evidence of plant and insect remains from the watercourses indicates weedy open grassland in the more immediate vicinity and suggests that cattle were pastured and watered at the backs of the plots. This is not too surprising given that both the Edgbaston Street and northeastern market-place plots backed directly onto parkland at this time. Significantly, the discovery of plant remains that have been interpreted as being indicative of charred fodder in the ditch on the northeastern side of the market place further points to the corralling of cattle here, awaiting resale at the market or, more probably, slaughter. In the 13th century there is also evidence of domestic occupation behind the Edgbaston Street plot frontage, in the form of a possible kiln, drying oven and some sort of water tank. Unfortunately the fact that the modern streets have been widened to accommodate extra people and motorised traffic meant that at no point was it possible to get a look at a medieval frontage.

Early expansion

The archaeological evidence shows that the creation of Moor Street and Park Street belongs to a phase of expansion of the medieval town, probably in the 13th century but possibly in the early 14th century. Moor Street may be slightly earlier than Park Street. The slightly curving profile of these streets is probably caused by their following two roughly equidistant contour lines along the sandstone ridge. Their construction altered the drainage system on this side of the market, involving the probable downgrading of some old watercourses to culverts but also the cutting of new ones to service the newly created plots. Might this have affected the occupation and trade profile of the old plots fronting onto the market, with a shift away from production or, in the case of animals, stock watering towards more exclusively commercial and trading functions?

The name 'Park Street' (occasionally 'Little Park Street') reminds us that this street was laid out over one of the lord's hunting parks, variously called Little Park or Over Park. This strongly suggests the direct involvement of the de Birmingham lords in this phase of urban expansion. Apparently, for the de Birminghams, the pursuit of profit was more pressing than the pursuit of game!

CM

A medieval lead weight from Park Street.

We also have evidence for early expansion of the town in the form of 'ribbon development' along Digbeth. Eighteenth-century maps show a great snaking band of burgage plots down Digbeth to the River Rea, and up again into Deritend (or 'Deer-gate-end' – the name recalling the eastern boundary of the Lord of Birmingham's hunting parks) and Bordesley. Here, however, we encounter a complication, because when we cross the River Rea we cross from the parish and original manor of Birmingham into the ancient parish of Aston, and into what must originally have been a separate manor. The market street through Deritend may not, in fact, be the furthest and latest extension from the central area of medieval Birmingham. Instead, it may have been launched by the lord of Aston around the same time as the lord of Birmingham was developing his market, in a deliberate attempt to divert some of the trade from Birmingham and capture a neighbours' profits. Fierce commercial competition is not a recent phenomenon! If this was so, no later than the 1270s Deritend was acquired by the energetic de Birmingham family, who began to impose their own market tolls there, in effect incorporating Deritend into Birmingham.

Industry, trade and the character of medieval Birmingham

The first archaeological evidence for industrial activity begins to appear in the 12th century around the Bull Ring, including tanning behind Edgbaston Street and metal working in the Moor Street and Park Street excavations. At the Park Street site there was also kiln debris and a scatter of wasters from pottery production. While we have to be careful of bias in the archaeological record – certain industries such as pottery production, tanning and metal working tending to leave more immediately recognisable evidence than others – the type of activity and its relative visibility may be usefully compared with the documentary evidence available.

Probably the most definitive interpretation to date of the albeit extremely scanty documentation for the early history of the town is that written by Richard Holt in 1985. Here he sharply attacks the views of Conrad Gill, author of the first volume of the official *History of Birmingham* published in 1952. Gill was of the opinion that as Birmingham did not possess a formal borough charter (indeed did not possess one until the 19th century) it could not have been a town but merely a village: 'Birmingham was throughout the medieval period, and indeed much of the 16th century, a village, a community based on the practice of agriculture that contained a market and a small group of merchants, but in which manufacturing was of little importance'. Instead, Holt argues that while we have, indeed, an insignificant and purely agricultural settlement depicted in the Domesday survey of 1086, by the 16th century this had transformed itself into a community 'wherein, although agriculture remained an important element in the economy of the town, this was of minor importance compared with the manufacturing and trade activities taking place here'. He goes further to argue that the pace of this change was not gradual, but that from around the time of the granting of the market charter in 1166 Birmingham's take off was in fact rapid, in common with what was happening in many places up and down England. For example, in the reconfirmation of the market charter made in 1189, the location of the market is defined as being in the town and not by the '*castrum*' any more. By the 1250s there was sufficient money to rebuild the church, and the usual reason for action such as this was that the old one was no longer appropriate, either in terms of the size or the status of the population it served. In 1275 the town was also represented at an unusual Parliament, qualifying specifically because of its reputation as a merchant town or '*villate mercatum*'. Solihull, a town founded slightly later than Birmingham, actually went as far as to use the privileges enjoyed by burgesses of Birmingham as a model for themselves.

The extremely fragmentary historical documentation means that it is very difficult to get a clear picture of the occupations of the inhabitants of Birmingham in the medieval period. The occupations of half of the 16 townspeople who negotiated release from the duty of helping with the lord's haymaking in 1232 are identifiable. They comprised a 'purveyor', a mercer, a smith, a tailor and four weavers. A weaver is mentioned in 1239 and in 1280 there is a reference to a dyer. The repeated references to those involved in the cloth industry is noteworthy, and the importance of the cloth trade is also shown in tax returns on cloth sales in the closing years of the 14th century, which show Birmingham as the second largest cloth market in Warwickshire (after Coventry, which is massively out in front). The historical record also provides some evidence of the importance of the cattle trade in medieval Birmingham, mainly through cases of evasions of tolls that came to trial, but these belong to the early 15th century.

How does the new archaeological evidence affect our picture of medieval Birmingham and what does it tell us about the character of the settlement? Bearing in mind the fact that we have, as yet, only a few pieces from a complex jigsaw puzzle, the archaeological evidence is surprisingly informative. Against a background of everyday agricultural activities it tells us, first, of a vigorous trade in cattle and of thriving industry associated with the products of cattle, notably leather working. It also tells us, second, of the existence of other industry, notably pottery production for which there is no historical evidence. Third, it shows us the importance of the water supply in influencing the layout of the town and its economy. Fourth, it tells us – the development of Moor Street and Park Street is the crucial piece of evidence here – that the town was expanding up until the 14th century. Fifth, it affords insights into environmental conditions within the town and the nature of the surrounding countryside. And sixth, it provides us with information on the location of various activities within the town and some detail of their physical character.

With regard to the last two points, it is noteworthy that industrial processes such as tanning and pottery making, which are smelly at best, were carried out in close proximity to the market centre. Elsewhere such antisocial activities were generally banished to the outskirts of town. It is worth remembering in this context that it took our 19th-century forebears in Birmingham some fifty years to begin to seriously grapple with the social and environmental consequences of rapid industrialisation, and they were dealing with a problem on an altogether different scale.

The apparent importance of the cloth industry in medieval Birmingham, suggested by documentary sources, is not directly reflected in the archaeological record. This returns us to the point about the variable visibility of different activities in the archaeological record. Pottery production leaves substantial and generally unequivocal evidence in the archaeological record; activities associated with the cloth industry, such as weaving, fulling and dyeing often leave much more ephemeral and equivocal traces. The clay-lined pits or tanks uncovered at Park Street could be associated with textile production, as we speculated in the last chapter, but positively identifying such activities in the archaeological record for Birmingham remains a challenge for the future.

Why was Medieval Birmingham a success?

The archaeological and historical evidence we have reviewed demonstrate beyond reasonable doubt that from its receipt of a market charter in 1166 the market town of Birmingham was a success and expanded rapidly. By 1300 Birmingham had outstripped in size and wealth all the other manors of the Birmingham area. The time has come to ask the question – why?

After all, on the face of things the manor of Birmingham did not have that much going for it. At the time of the Domesday survey (1086) it was valued at only £1; Birmingham was not blessed with good soil for agriculture. The site chosen to develop the market town was, as we have seen, a good one in terms of communications and water supply, but plenty of the manors in the surrounding area were as well if not better provided.

The answer seems to have three ingredients – necessity, entrepreneurial flair and timing. An ambitious lord of Birmingham (and the de Birmingham family was clearly ambitious) could not make his fortune from agriculture – the land was too poor. So it was necessary to take another route to getting rich, and that was trade. Laying out the market town, buying the market charter, encouraging people to settle in the town and even buying out rivals who were too close for comfort (as may have been the case with an early independent market at Deritend) all required substantial investment and a good degree of entrepreneurial flair. Peter de Birmingham and his family evidently had what it takes. They derived their income – the return on this investment – primarily in the form of rents, market tolls and fines. We repeatedly see evidence of the hand of the de Birmingham family in advancing the development of Birmingham and protecting their investment.

The third ingredient – timing – is perhaps the most important, and obviously not unrelated to business acumen. The period from the Domesday survey of 1086 to 1300 was a time of great expansion. The population of England probably trebled or more. All over the Midlands the villages and towns were expanding, new hamlets and farmsteads sprang up, some in clearings laboriously made in the forest (many of the medieval moated sites of the Birmingham area began in this way), and new fields were carved out of the waste. Sophisticated market research was not needed to recognise the opportunity this presented to those willing and able to seize it. The market charter that Peter de Birmingham purchased in 1166 was the earliest for the whole of the Birmingham Plateau. Quite simply, Birmingham got in there first and by the time its immediate rivals – Sutton, Coleshill, Solihull, Bromsgrove, Halesowen, Dudley, Wednesbury, Walsall – had got their act together people had already got into the habit of trading at Birmingham. From then on, success bred success.

Chapter 5

A Good Market Town

From receiving its market charter in 1166 down to the end of the 13th century, the archaeological and historical evidence points to the growth of Birmingham to become the most important market centre on the Birmingham plateau, outstripping its rivals. However, the seeds of Birmingham's growth to become a town of national importance lie in the 15th and 16th centuries, when Birmingham takes on an increasingly industrial character specialising in ironworking.

In this chapter we will explore this period of transition, mixing history with the new perspective provided by the Bull Ring excavations. First, however, we must start with the 14th century, a period of apparent decline.

Decline and recovery

The history of Birmingham cannot be divorced from the wider history of Britain and Europe. Birmingham's growth in the 12th and 13th centuries was mirrored by a national growth in population that peaked in the second half of the 13th century. Indeed, the rising rural population around Birmingham was undoubtedly a major factor that drove the growth of the market town.

By the end of the 13th century the growth of England's population and economy was beginning to flag; given the farming techniques of the time, population growth had probably reached the limits of the available resources – many were at or below the poverty line, easy victims to famine and disease. Then, beginning in the early 14th century, a long, slow disaster unfolded. Exceptionally bad weather in the opening decades of the century led to a series of poor harvests, with widespread crop failure in 1315 and 1316 (sometimes called the 'Great Famine'), 1320 and 1321. Grain prices soared and tens of thousands died of starvation. To make matters worse, sheep and cattle murrains (infectious diseases) struck in 1313-17 and 1319-21 respectively.

Locally, Halesowen Manor provides an example of the extent of the crisis: in 1315-16 grain prices increased five-fold and in 1315-17 fifteen percent of the male population died, no doubt a simple case of cause and effect. Even closer to hand, the population of Yardley, which had been around 800 in 1275, had dropped to around 600 by 1327.

The process of decline was complicated and uneven – as in any crisis there were winners and losers – and during the 1320s and 30s there may have been a temporary

Burial of plague victims in the 14th century.

recovery. Then disaster struck again when the Black Death (bubonic plague) appeared in southern England in 1348, spreading as far as central Scotland by 1349. At a stroke, England's population was reduced by about a third. A contemporary writer, Geoffrey le Baker, described the effects: 'This great pestilence … raged for a whole year in England so terribly that it cleared many country villages entirely of every human being'. He also wrote, 'As the graveyards did not suffice, fields were chosen for the burial of the dead'. Could it just be that we have here another possible explanation for the mysterious burials at Park Street described in Chapter 3 – victims of the Black Death afforded burial at Park Street because the graveyard of St. Martin's simply couldn't cope?

England's market towns, many of which like Birmingham had sprung up in the 12th and 13th centuries, were badly affected by the crisis. In Warwickshire – Birmingham's county – there were about 34 market towns in 1300; by 1500 there were about half this many. Birmingham was one of the survivors, but it can hardly have gone unscathed. One of the most striking things to emerge from Stephanie Rátkai's study of the pottery from the Bull Ring excavations is how little is attributed to the 14th century – the decline of the town seems almost tangible in the pottery from the excavations. As if disasters on a national scale were not enough, a local disaster seems to have struck Birmingham around 1300. This was the great fire of Birmingham. Such is the poverty of historical documentation for medieval Birmingham that we only know of this fire incidentally, from the records of a court case that took place at Halesowen in 1313. A key document relevant to the case had been destroyed some years previously in 'the big fire of the town of Birmingham' (*magnum combustionem ville de Birmigham*). In Chapter 3 we saw how Stephanie Rátkai speculated that the contents of a pit which seemed to represent the debris from a house fire may have been associated with the great fire.

Nevertheless, Birmingham rode out the crises at both the national and local level. The reduced population had made some farmers rich, as they bought up unwanted acres and built up big estates. A new class of very wealthy 'yeoman' farmers emerged. Furthermore, with less mouths to feed less corn was needed and the local farmers focussed increasingly on cattle rearing to turn a profit. And as animal husbandry is less labour intensive than cultivating crops, this freed up labour for craft and industry. Out of this mix the recovery of Birmingham's prosperity was built: a vibrant cattle market, wealthy customers demanding a wide range of goods, and a free labour force to provide them.

Already too, from as early as the beginning of the 14th century, Birmingham had a reputation for its manufactures. Evidence for this comes from an unlikely source. In 1308 the Knights Templar were subjected to mass arrests on trumped up charges of heresy, obscene practices, homosexuality and so forth. The master of the Order, William de la More, was imprisoned and an inventory of his property was made. The inventory includes eleven 'Birmingham pieces' worth 22s. What these pieces were we can only speculate, but their high value suggests metal objects of good craftsmanship. The important point is that 'Birmingham piece' already meant something to people, even in London.

The noise of anvils

The traveller John Leland visited Birmingham in 1538 and wrote an oft-quoted description of the town. Here is part of it:

> *'The beauty of Bermingham, a good markett towne in the extreame parts of Warwikshire, is one street goinge up alonge .... a meane hill, by the length of a quarter of a mile. I saw but one Parroch Churche in the towne. There be many*

smiths in the towne that use to make knives and all mannour of cutting tooles, and many lorimers that make bittes and a great many naylors. Soe that a great part of the towne is maintained by smithes, who have their iron and sea-cole out of Staffordshire.'

The one street going up a hill is, of course, Digbeth and the parish church St. Martin's. What impressed Leland, and indeed all other visitors, was the extent of Birmingham's ironworking industry, but other documentary sources – which become much richer from this time onwards – mention many other trades, and prominent amongst these are the cloth and leather industries. The Bull Ring excavations provided tangible evidence of several of these trades, and below we will briefly review developments in the 15th and 16th centuries in our three 'jigsaw puzzle pieces' – the Edgbaston Street, Moor Street and Park Street sites.

Old smithy and open forge in Digbeth.

The archaeological evidence for industry

Edgbaston Street

The Edgbaston Street tannery established in the medieval period expanded in the 15th and 16th centuries. Older pits were cleared out and reused and at least six new pits were dug. Three tools were uncovered which were possibly associated with leather working: a possible hide-scraping tool made from horncore, a worked bone handle and a whetstone. Leather off-cuts provided further evidence of the manufacturing process, and 'bark scleroids' and 'bark beetles' from the pits attested to the use of bark to produce the tanning liquor.

Moor Street

In the small area excavated at Moor Street the main evidence for this period comprised a series of rubbish pits. The contents of the pits, several of which contained a high concentration of charcoal, suggested continued industrial activity on the site.

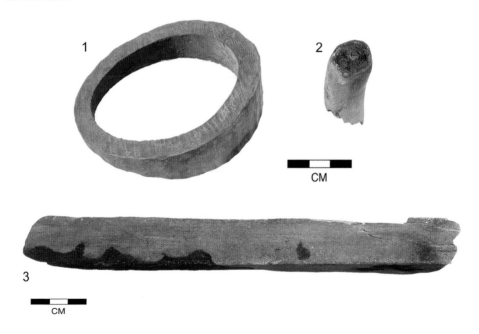

Possible leather working tools from Edgbaston Street. 1 – a possible hide-scraping tool made from a horncore; 2 – a worked bone handle fitted with a copper-alloy bar; 3 – a stone worn to a smooth gloss, possibly from rubbing leather.

Park Street

At Park Street, industrial activity continued, most clearly represented by the digging of a further series of large clay-lined pits or tanks at the rear of the plots. Water storage was indicated not only by the size, shape and construction of the tanks, but also by the waterlogged soils found filling them. Hemp and flax seeds from these pits suggested textile processing, an activity which continued from the medieval period. The waterlogged fills of the pits

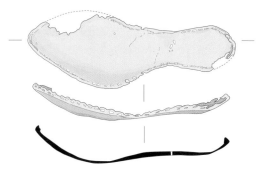

The sole of a leather shoe from the Park Street site.

preserved a good range of artefacts, including pieces of leather and the sole of a shoe.

Other pits provided evidence of continued metalworking on the site, in the form of slag and coal. Iron nails, copper alloy objects, pottery, tile and animal bones were found amongst the rubbish. Another indication of high-temperature industrial activity was provided by the survival of a kiln cut into the ground in a keyhole shape. However, there was no clear evidence of what this kiln was used for.

A kiln on the Park Street site. The kiln has a characteristic 'keyhole' shape but there were no clues to its use.

The character of the town

The archaeological evidence from the Bull Ring sites suggests that a major theme of the 15th and 16th centuries was continuity from the medieval period. At Edgbaston Street, Moor Street and Park Street the old industries – tanning, textile working, ironworking – continue and possibly intensify. There also seems to be less emphasis on the agricultural pursuits that were apparent from the plant remains found in the ditches and pits of the medieval period.

While retaining much of its medieval character, therefore, the town was becoming more industrial. This does not mean that factories employing hundreds of workers were springing up – these belong to an altogether later era. Industry in Birmingham – whether tanning or smithing – was a small-scale, household affair and continued alongside the town's other major function, that of being a regional market for livestock, produce and goods of all types.

When John Leland in 1538 wrote that 'a great part of the town is maintained by smithes', or when William Camden in 1563 found the place 'swarming with inhabitants and echoing with the noise of anvils', what they were describing were not great enterprises but a multitude of small businesses, usually just the craftsman and his family with occasionally perhaps one or two employees. The work took place in the family house or its backyard. Indeed, setting up as a smith was fairly easy – which is no doubt why so many chose to do so – and required little capital investment; at the time Leland was writing an adequate set of smith's tools, including anvil, bellows and hammers, could probably be bought for less than 10s. The Park Street smiths whose activities have been documented by archaeological excavation can be supposed to be small-scale craftsmen of this type. Many, especially nailors and the like, were probably 'dependent' craftsmen, in the sense that while they worked from their own homes and used their own tools, they were nevertheless tied by debt to an employer – an ironmonger – who controlled their work.

If smithing was an activity that could be readily entered into by the lower social groups, tanners tended to be men of more substance; we know this from surviving wills and inventories of the 16th century which show them to have been prosperous tradesmen. One cause of this distinction was that tanning was a slow process where the return on one's initial investment could be long delayed, a circumstance which tends to exclude the small operator. Indeed, it seems – again from wills and inventories – that a tanner would have to have around half of his wealth invested in hides if he was to manage to stay in business.

The Edgbaston Street tannery uncovered by archaeological excavation was probably the concern of one of these more prosperous independent tradesmen (although still essentially a family business). We have seen that the scale of the operation appears to have grown in the 15th and 16th centuries.

However, at this period the majority of the wealthiest people in Birmingham were not directly involved with industrial production but got their wealth from land, cattle or trade. An analysis of tax figures for 1525 shows that just 9% of those liable to pay tax, only fourteen persons, owned 50% of the wealth of the town. The occupations of these fourteen persons are instructive: they comprised Edward de Birmingham (the lord of the manor), a grazier, a grazier's widow, a mercer, a mercer's widow, a lawyer, two ironmongers, a tanner and a scythesmith, and three whose occupations are unknown. We should not, therefore, overestimate the importance of industry in general or ironworking in particular in Birmingham's economy at this time. Nevertheless it was of growing significance.

In the previous chapter we posed the question of why Birmingham amongst all the villages on the Birmingham plateau developed to become the pre-eminent local market town. We should now ask the question, what factors explain the growth of industry, and especially ironworking, in the town in the 15th and 16th centuries?

One factor we can probably eliminate is the hand of the de Birmingham family, however important the early lords may have been in the establishment and early development of the town. Edward de Birmingham, who headed the tax list of 1525 mentioned above, was soon to be in deep trouble. He had made enemies in court, was arrested and had his property confiscated, spent the years 1533 to 1537 in the Tower of London and, although eventually released, was dead by 1538. This ended the long association of the de Birmingham family with the manor and town of Birmingham. The manor had passed into the hands of the Crown, which later disposed of it, but none of the subsequent lords of the manor seem to have had any significant influence on the development of the town.

The key factor was the proximity of Birmingham to the South Staffordshire coalfield and the iron and coal resources of the Black Country. The rise of the Staffordshire iron industry and Birmingham's industrial development went hand in hand. Put simply, Birmingham happened to be in the right place at the right time, positioned between the coalfield to the northwest, from where it got its raw materials, and lucrative markets for its products to the south and east (although the bulk of its trade remained local at this period). Furthermore, Birmingham benefited from its existing status as a vigorous market with good communications.

Ironically, a third factor may have been that Birmingham then lacked the status of a chartered town – a market charter had been sought and granted but not a town charter. This gave a certain freedom to the development of trade and industry which was not fettered by a restrictive guild system with antiquated privileges and exclusive apprenticeship regulations. In the words of Birmingham's first historian, William Hutton, 'A town without a charter is a town without a shackle'. A man could migrate into Birmingham from the surrounding regions and set up as, say, a smith with comparative ease, as hundreds evidently did; the population of Birmingham was both growing and changing in character. It was not, however, until the end of the 17th and the beginning of the 18th century that Birmingham broke with its medieval past and became altogether more than just a 'good markett towne'. This radical transformation, which is richly reflected in the archaeological record of the Bull Ring sites, is the subject of the next chapter.

Chapter 6

Transformation

Victorian Birmingham was a town so different from the medieval and Tudor market town that it can be hard to see any connection between the two. The growth in the size of the town (it only became a city in 1889) and its population was staggering. A reasonable estimate of the population of Birmingham in 1700 is in the region of 5,000 to 7,000; in 1837, the year of Queen Victoria's accession, it was about 170,000 and by 1901, the year of Victoria's death, it was over 500,000.

Nothing quite like this had happened before in the history of the world. Of course, other provincial centres – Leeds, Manchester, Liverpool and Glasgow – experienced a similar transformation, but the interrelated developments of industrial revolution, population growth and the massive growth of her industrial towns and cities was something happening in Britain for the first time ever, and Birmingham was in the vanguard of the process.

In the early stages of its transformation, Birmingham's growth was fundamentally unplanned and out of control. It was all so unprecedented that history had no lessons to offer, and in any case the essentially medieval civic institutions of the town lacked the structure or resources to exercise any kind of meaningful control. Moreover, in many influential circles there was little political will to intervene – a *laissez faire* philosophy prevailed.

With the benefit of hindsight the long-term results of such uncontrolled growth seem predictable. By the opening years of the 19th century the older parts of the town – the areas around the Bull Ring – had become hopelessly overcrowded and started down the relentless spiral into slumdom. In the absence of piped water or sewage systems (which require civic will and resources) the sanitary conditions were often appalling. The air was black and poisoned with the smoke from thousands of chimneys. In the squalor, people died in their thousands.

The first Bull Ring redevelopment

Of course, it was not that nothing was eventually done, although it was often a case of 'too little, too late'. In 1769 a local Act of Parliament established a group of officials known as the 'Improvement or Street Commissioners', responsible for the planning of streets, lighting, pollution, crime and housing. They were also charged with sorting out Birmingham's old medieval market place, which had become terribly congested, with trading activity spilling out into the surrounding streets. The

The Bull Ring market place in the later 18th century. In the foreground is the Old Cross; the chamber over the cross was built in 1703 and demolished in 1784. Behind is St. Martin's Church, which is surrounded by timber-framed shops that had encroached onto the market place; these buildings were cleared away by the Street Commissioners at the end of the 18th century. Note the tall, thin buildings fronting onto the market place, some of which are still of medieval character.

contemporary historian, William Hutton, described the problem: 'The space now used as our market was in 1769 completely choked with buildings and filth; the shambles, the round house and the cross nearly filled the area'. The Commissioners cleared the market space – the Old Cross was demolished in 1784 and by 1810 the process was largely complete. They also provided new market facilities. The site of the Birmingham Moat was bought, cleared and the moat filled in between 1815 and 1817. On 5th April 1817 a 'New Beast Market' – Smithfield Market – was opened on the site. After the market opened it became an offence to 'expose to Sale any Cattle, Horses, Sheep and Pigs, Hay or Straw, in any other Part of the said Town'. Next the Commissioners turned their attention to getting the bulk of the Bull Ring's retail marketing off the streets. This led to the demolition of many of the buildings

The Birmingham Moat and Manor House c.1815, on the eve of its destruction to create Smithfield Market. Note the spire of St. Martin's church in the background.

fronting onto the west side of the old market place and the erection of the Market Hall, opened in 1835. At the time it was claimed to be 'the finest building of the kind in the kingdom'; 600 stalls could be 'accommodated in the body of the hall, and space left for four thousand persons to perambulate'.

We can see these events as the first Bull Ring redevelopment, a process which continued piecemeal into the later 19th century with the construction of St. Martin's Market, a wholesale butcher's market in 1851, a wholesale fish market (1869) and a covered vegetable market (1884). It was a redevelopment appropriate to its time, just as the 1960s redevelopment and the new Bullring are appropriate to their time.

The Market Hall, opened in 1835, photographed on the occasion of its centenary in 1935.

History and archaeology

We can appreciate from the few details given in the previous section that from the 18th century onwards there is a wealth of historical documentation relating to the political, economic and social development of Birmingham. In this well-documented period archaeology adopts the role of providing a new perspective on a familiar story, and providing a new type of evidence which may variously reinforce, illuminate or challenge that story. The excavations at Edgbaston Street and Park Street have provided the first opportunity to look at the transformation of Birmingham from an archaeological perspective, in two of the oldest parts of the town. Compared to the size of Birmingham by the late 18th century the size of the two sites is miniscule. To return to an earlier analogy, they are two tiny pieces in a 5,000-piece jigsaw puzzle, so we cannot expect them to give us more than a fraction of the picture. Nevertheless, some important new evidence has emerged, together with a wide range of finds which give material expression to this fundamental period of Birmingham's history. Before we take a look at this new evidence, however, we need to sketch out the historical outlines of Birmingham's industrial and physical development in the 17th and 18th centuries, which provides a framework within which the archaeological evidence can be interpreted.

The 17th century: a slow fuse

In terms of the industrial development of Birmingham, we can perhaps think of the 17th century as a slow fuse, sparking a detonator bomb around the end of the 17th century, which in turn ignited the full explosion in the latter part of the 18th century.

In the 17th century, the old trades continued, with ironworking foremost amongst them. The hearth tax returns of 1683 reveal that there were 202 forges in Birmingham, more than half of them to be found in Edgbaston Street, Digbeth and Deritend. The emphasis was on the production of swords, edge tools such as scythes, and nails. Indeed, according to tradition it was the sword production of one Robert Porter, who had a blade mill on the River Rea, that contributed to provoking Prince Rupert into the sacking of the town (and the destruction of the offending mill) in the 'Battle of Birmingham' of 1643, briefly described in Chapter 3. It was alleged that Porter had supplied the Parliamentary army with 15,000 swords.

To the making of all manner of iron items, the craftsmen of Birmingham added two important industries in the 17th century, the working of brass (copper mixed with zinc) and the making of guns, with the manufacture of flint-lock guns and pistols well established by the 1680s. This diversification into new materials and new manufactures was the fuse that sparked a small explosion in production around the end of the century.

Nevertheless, if we were to compare the Birmingham of 1650 with the Birmingham of 1250, on the one hand, and the Birmingham of 1750 on the other hand, we would probably find more in common with the former than the latter. 'The ancient and modern state of Birmingham must divide at the restoration of Charles the Second' (1660), wrote William Hutton in 1781. Up until then, Hutton believed, smiths were Birmingham's 'chief inhabitants' and 'the chief if not the only manufactory ... was in iron'. After the Restoration, 'many of the curious manufactures began to blossom'.

The early 18th century: detonation

This was a period of very rapid population growth in Birmingham; indeed, it may have been the fastest growing industrial town in the country. In 1700 Birmingham probably had a population of between 5,000 and 7,000 but by 1750 the population had at least trebled in size to 23,688. This was at a time when the population of England has only increased by about 14%, and even other industrial towns such as Leeds and Manchester had only about doubled in size.

This huge increase in population had an obvious impact on the fabric and character of the town. In 1750 it was claimed of Birmingham that, 'this place has been for a long series of years increasing in its buildings' – much of Birmingham had been turned into a building site (a familiar enough story for today's reader!). The effect of all this building changed the character of the town. Expansion took place to the north and west of the old medieval town, up onto the sandstone ridge on which Birmingham sits, with new estates being laid out by speculative developers. The town could now be divided into an old lower area, focussing on Digbeth and the Bull Ring market place, mainly industrial in character and retaining many old timber-framed buildings, and a new upper area, more residential in character and mainly composed of new brick buildings. This division was noted by a London visitor in 1755, who described Birmingham as

> '... *another London in miniature: it stands on the Side of a Hill, forming a Half-moon; the lower part is filled with the Workshops and Ware-houses of the manufacturers, and consists chiefly of old Buildings; the Upper Part of the Town, like St James's, contains a Number of new, regular streets, and a handsome square, all well-built and well-inhabited ...*'

This transformation can be well appreciated from Bradford's map of 1751. The grid of new, regular streets – only partially developed – can be clearly seen to the northwest of the old town. The 'handsome square' to which the 1755 visitor refers is marked as 'The Square' (later the Old Square), for a while one of the best addresses in Birmingham. Yet the familiar landmarks of the medieval town are all still there – the long ribbon development of old properties up Digbeth, the

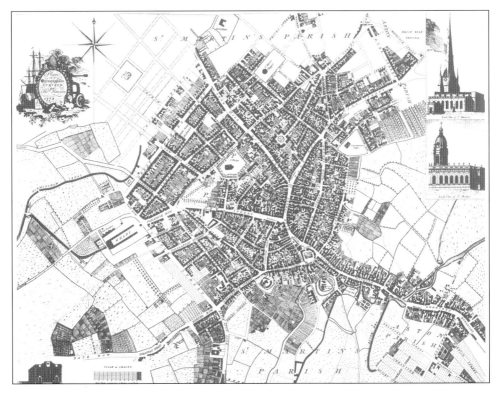

Bradford's 1751 map of the town. By this date the town has expanded substantially to the north and west of the old centre, with a grid of streets around St. Paul's awaiting further development.

Birmingham Moat and the Parsonage Moat, and, of course, the triangular Bull Ring market place with St. Martin's church. The market place has still not been freed of the clutter of buildings that had encroached upon it.

Fuelling Birmingham's first phase of growth and transformation in the early 18th century was the development of the toy trade; in the latter part of the century the trade was to explode.

The late 18th century: an explosion in the toy trade

When Edmund Burke famously described Birmingham in 1777 as 'the great toyshop of Europe', he was not referring to children's playthings. 'Toys', in the sense that Burke used the term, refers to great variety of small articles of iron, brass and steel, such as utensils, household fittings, buckles, buttons, snuff boxes, and trinkets and knick-knacks of all kinds. These are what Hutton meant by the 'curious manufactures' of the 'modern state' of Birmingham. It was upon the toy trade that much of Birmingham's prosperity was built in the 18th century.

Several factors have been singled out to explain the success of Birmingham's toy trade, although not all were contemporary. The import of new materials, notable brass, into Birmingham was one factor. Another factor was the skill with which the Birmingham ironsmiths could adapt their traditional techniques and equipment to meet new demands.

Towards the middle of the 18th century, a third factor was certainly the way in which labour was organised and divided. Of the manufacture of buttons, the London visitor of 1755 who we met earlier observed:

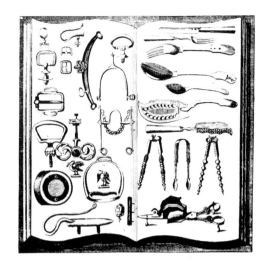

Typical Birmingham 'toys' – from an advertisement in Wrightson's New Triennial Directory of Birmingham, 1818.

> *'The Multitude of Hands each Button goes thro' before it is sent to the Market is likewise surprising; you will perhaps think it incredible when I tell you they go thro' 70 different Operations of 70 different Work-folk.'*

This organisation of labour reached its peak at the famous Soho Manufactory of Matthew Boulton, built at Handsworth in 1764 and employing up to a thousand workers, but this belongs to a developed stage of the toy trade. Operations in the old part of Birmingham, such as Edgbaston Street or Park Street, at the end of the 17th century and in the early 18th century would have been much simpler. Matthew Boulton's own family history illustrates this – his father (also called Matthew) was, in the early years of the 18th century, a small Birmingham buckle and button maker.

A fourth factor credited with explaining the success of the Birmingham toy industry was the employment of machinery. In 1770 Matthew Boulton claimed that at his Soho manufactory

> *'... by the many mechanical contrivances and extensive apparatus wh we are possess'd of, our men are enabled to do from twice to ten times the work that can be done without the help of such contrivances & even women and children do more than men can do without them.'*

Despite Boulton's later reputation and his famous partnership with James Watt in the development of the steam engine, the 'mechanical contrivances' which drove the toy industry were not generally great engines but small, hand-operated machines. Chief amongst them were the stamp, the press, the lathe and the drawbench. In its basic form, none of this technology was new in the 18th century.

With this briefest of historical sketches providing a framework for our investigations, let's now turn to the archaeological evidence for Birmingham's transformation, as found in the Bull Ring excavations. What insights and new perspectives can it provide?

Edgbaston Street

An expanding tannery

At our Edgbaston Street site we witness, not the demise of the tanning industry to be replaced by metalworking associated with the toy industry, but a major expansion of leatherworking activity in the 17th century. In the area of the old tannery, first established in the medieval period, at least five new pits were dug. One of these, a circular pit, was filled with lime. Close to the watercourse was a second pit containing lime; it was wood lined – or possibly represented the remains of a sunken wooden barrel – and was found with its wooden lid preserved in position. Lime, as we shall see below, played an essential role in the early stages of the tanning process. Elsewhere in the area of the old tannery a series of slots were dug to channel water, or tanning liquid, into a large tanning pit. The soils filling two other pits, on the fringes of the area, contained in one case large quantities of preserved wood and leather off-cuts (including a fragment of a shoe) and in the other a concentration of cattle horncores.

While the old tannery continued in business, probably through to the end of the 17th century, new operations opened up in a plot to the east. These may be interpreted as either an expansion of the old business or the opening of a new business; whatever the case, the scale of the industry was on the increase. In the new area, where leather preparation took place for the first time in the 17th century, the layout of the pits followed a regular pattern. A series of nine roughly rectangular pits was laid out in a line following the generally north-south alignment of the burgage plot. The small size of the pits suggests they may they may have been used to cure the hides rather than tan them, which may – if it was all part of one expanded business – still have taken place in the old tannery to the west. All of the pits had been filled with similar deposits of compacted ground wood chips or sawdust. To one side of the line of putative leather curing pits were

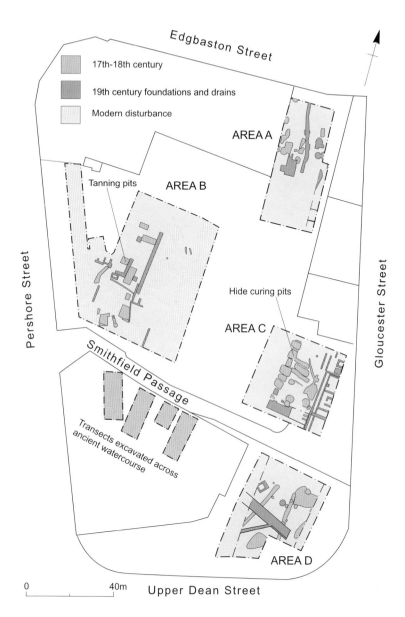

A plan of the Edgbaston Street site showing archaeological remains from the 17th to the early 19th century. In the 17th and early 18th century the tanning industry reaches its greatest extent on the site, with new pits dug in the eastern part of the site (Area C) and activity extending for the first time to the south of the watercourse (Area D). Also in the eastern part of the site, walls were uncovered probably belonging to Welch's Skin Yard.

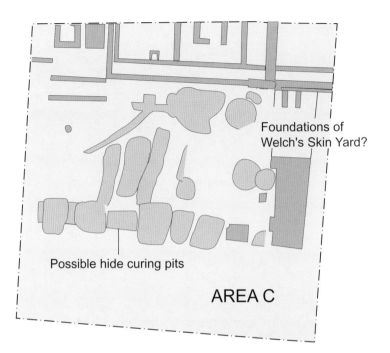

Foundations of
Welch's Skin Yard?

Possible hide curing pits

AREA C

Plan and photograph of 17th-century tanning pits uncovered in Area C of the Edgbaston Street site. The row of possible hide-curing pits is at the bottom/foreground with walls probably belonging to the later Welch's Skin Yard above/behind.

three elongated pits which had been re-cut on several occasions, suggesting repeated emptying and refilling. They also contained fillings of decomposed ground wood chips with occasional leather fragments, and are interpreted as pits used to drain waste material from the curing pits. The partial skeletons of two new-born puppies were also found in one of these pits; harsh though it may sound, the most likely interpretation is that they were unwanted and destroyed at birth. They are a reminder that all sorts of 'rubbish' was disposed of in the pits once they had fallen into disuse.

Thus the tanning industry expanded considerably in the 17th century. In addition to the putative curing pits and waste pits already described, tanning activity was represented by a further linear arrangement of pits, two wells (which would have provided an additional source of water to the watercourse) and a cobbled tanning yard. Furthermore, for the first time industrial activity expanded south of the watercourse linking the Parsonage Moat and the Birmingham Moat, into an area which had long remained outside the built up area of the town. Here was found a number of pits, together with gullies and postholes suggesting the erection of timber outbuildings. The ground was wet here, and bands of crushed coke probably represent an attempt to build up and consolidate the wet ground.

The tanning process

The range of pits with their different fillings, together with other features found to the south of Edgbaston Street, provide evidence of several of the stages involved in the process of making leather. Using traditional methods, this was a long process, taking up to two years. First the hides were suspended in pits containing solutions of lime in order to loosen the hair and outer tissues. Then a special knife was used to remove the loosened material. The hides were then made supple using infusions of birds' or dogs' dung. After this preparation, the tanning itself took place. The hides were first tanned in a weak solution of oak bark, then in liquors of increasing strength, in each of which they might remain for a month or more. The process concluded with the drying of the leather.

A contemporary illustration of an 18th-century tannery.

73

The Edgbaston Street leather workers

Despite the noxious character of tanning and other aspects of leather preparation and working, it is likely that in the 17th century and earlier the leather workers lived on the site and that this was a family business. The domestic residence would have been on the street frontage, with the tannery behind. Nothing remained of the houses on the street frontage, but there was a cluster of pits containing pottery and other domestic refuse immediately to the rear of where one of the houses would have stood.

These pits, together with the tanning and other industrial pits, seem to have been deliberately filled in with rubbish and soil at about the same time, probably around 1700-1725. This marks the end of this phase of activity on the site. The rubbish found in the infilling of the pits had presumably been standing around in midden heaps and so forth before it was tipped into the pits – its contents tell us something about the people who had lived and worked on the site and the activities they were engaged in.

The pottery found amongst the rubbish was probably that used by the leather workers themselves. There were some clear distinctions between the pottery found in different areas of the site. Towards the frontage, for example, there was a preponderance of tablewares, comprising mainly drinking vessels, usually in blackware, together with bowls in coarseware and yellow ware, and a few dishes. In the area of the tanning operations, on the other hand, there was a preponderance of utilitarian pottery, notably jars – these may have held the beverages used for refreshment during work.

As we have seen, tanners were a relatively affluent group, and this may explain the presence of imported Rhenish stonewares amongst the pottery, which were a marker of the bourgeoisie in the

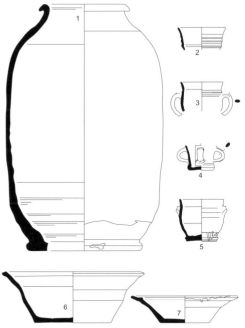

17th-century pottery from Edgbaston Street, when the tannery was at its height.
1 – Blackware jar; 2-4 – Blackware mugs;
5 – Yellow ware cup;
6 & 7 – Yellow ware bowls.

early post-medieval period. The presence of a fragment from the base of a wine glass and fragments of two possible marble floor tiles may tell a similar story.

The contents of the infilled pits and drains also provided other evidence of the activities carried out. Concentrations of cattle horncores are waste from the hides brought in for processing, as we have seen. The 17th-century horncores differed from those of the medieval period, representing mediumhorn 'breeds' rather than the shorthorn 'breeds' which dominated in the earlier period. Alongside meat and hides, horn and bone are other major products of animal carcasses. The evidence for horn and bone working amongst the rubbish mainly comprised debris from the manufacture of items, but there were one or two finished items also, including a comb.

Major reorganisation

We have seen that the pottery evidence indicates that the pits, drains and other 17th-century features on the site all seem to have been filled in in a deliberate operation around 1700-1725 or possibly a little earlier. This marks a major reorganisation of the site and a break with the more-or-less continuous industrial activity documented from the 13th century

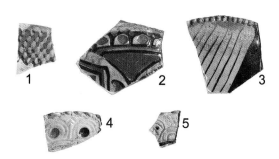

Late 17th-early 18th-century pottery from Edgbaston Street. 1 – Dish, brown and tan slip trellis design on rim; 2 – Base of dish, internal slip decoration; 3 – Dish, dark-on-light trailed slipware; 4 & 5 – Impressed slipware dishes. Note face decoration on no. 5.

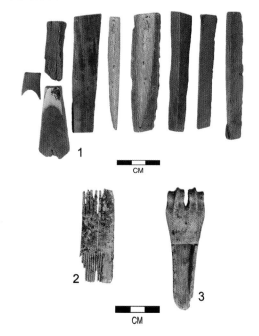

Debris from bone working at Edgbaston Street in the 17th century, with two finished items. 1 – Off-cuts from bone working; 2 – Bone comb; 3 – Scoop or corer.

onwards. Even more emphatic evidence of a break with the past is the accumulation across much of the site of a curious black 'cultivation soil' up to a metre in depth. Although the soil contained little pottery, what there was suggested that this phase of cultivation may have lasted for several decades in the middle years of the 18th century.

How are we to explain this curious phenomenon? A layer of 'dark earth', representing a phase of abandonment of buildings and the turning over of areas of towns to cultivation, is well-known to Roman archaeologists, where it is a feature of several Roman towns in the late Roman or sub Roman period. But the Birmingham 'dark earth' is not Roman but 18th century, and belongs to a period of rapid growth of the town!

Perhaps it is the association of Birmingham's 'dark earth' with a period of growth and transformation, as described in the earlier part of this chapter, that holds the key to its interpretation. While development was proceeding at a frenetic pace in the new areas of the town to the north and west of the old medieval centre, and the character and organisation of Birmingham's industries were changing along with residential patterns, building plots in the old parts of town, such as Edgbaston Street, fell temporarily vacant. However, the vacant plots would not have been simply abandoned, but would have been turned into gardens producing vegetables and the like for Birmingham's growing population and thriving market. The City Council's Planning Archaeologist, Mike Hodder, has suggested an attractive analogy. Today, when vacant plots in our town centres are awaiting development they are very often turned into temporary car parks – they meet a need and are a good means of making money from an empty space. In the 18th century needs were different and the empty spaces were turned into temporary market gardens.

Georgian grandeur and Welch's Skin Yard

However, such plots would not have remained vacant for long. By the middle of the 18th century a number of fine Queen Ann and Georgian brick houses lined Edgbaston Street, replacing the old timber-framed houses which had no doubt mainly lined the street up until the end of the 17th century. This can be seen on maps of the middle of the century and an advertisement of 1765 describes one of them:

> '... *handsome large commodious house, consisting of a large warehouse with a counting house behind it, two good parlours, a hall, two staircases, a china pantry, three large chambers, each having light and dark closet, many of each of them large enough to hold a bed, a spacious dining room, wainscoted, six good upper chambers with closets, a kitchen, pantry, four large cellars in one of which is a pump, a brewhouse with a pump, and an oven to bake bread, a good stable with a loft over it, a coach house and a large garden, with a canal, and other conveniences thereto belonging ...*'

(Notice the combination of accommodation for work and residence, and the facilities for brewing and baking, all on the same premises.) No such houses survived in the area of the excavation, but structures and finds relating to them did. To the rear of the frontage was a small cellar, from which was recovered a small collection of wine and beer glasses and fragments of oyster shells. An abandoned well nearby contained at least nine fine mid-late 18th-century creamware plates, some of which had clearly been complete when thrown into the well; they perhaps represent a house clearance.

The reference to a 'large garden' in the advertisement would help to explain the apparent longevity of the 'cultivation soil' found during the excavations; contemporary maps show many of the plots to the rear of the Edgbaston Street frontage occupied by gardens, some seemingly ornamental and others more functional.

Georgian grandeur – a 'Queen edge' creamware plate dating c. 1760-1780. The plate, one of at least nine, was dumped into a disused well in the early 19th century and may form part of a house clearance.

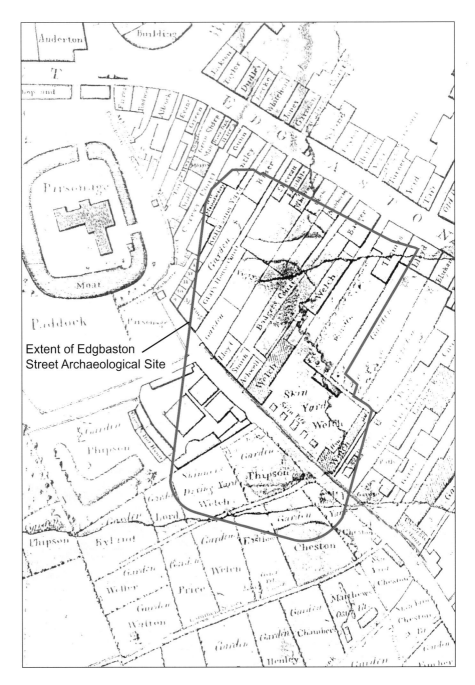

A map of 1808 showing Welch's Skin Yard occupying part of the Edgbaston Street site. The individual 'Skin Pits' are shown.

However, a typical 18th-century set up, again evident from the house advert, was still to mix residential buildings – even rather fine middle-class ones – with workshops. A map of 1808 shows that the eastern part of the excavated area was at that time occupied by Welch's Skin Yard (and even indicates the individual 'Skin Pits'), so despite all the changes, the tradition of preparing and working leather continued. It seems that the yard was established in the later 18th century and brick walls which were probably the foundations of parts of the buildings were uncovered by the excavations.

Slums and workshops

The relatively high status of Edgbaston Street during the later 18th century, indicated by the presence of substantial houses like the one described above, seems to have been short lived. The decline in the status of the area may have been in part a consequence of the establishment of Smithfield Market on the site of the old manorial moat in 1817. The destruction of the Parsonage Moat occurred in the same period, and with the obliteration of the two ancient moats the watercourse which had connected them was downgraded to an open sewer and later an underground sewer. Its approximate line was, however, preserved in Smithfield Passage.

As the population of Birmingham soared (it increased nine fold from about 24,000 in 1750 to around 220,000 in 1850) and industrialisation advanced, the middle classes abandoned 'inner city' areas such as Edgbaston Street and left their high-walled gardens to be filled up with small workshops and as much miserable working-class housing as could be crammed into them. These were the unsanitary 'courts', often situated behind the more substantial properties lining the street frontages. The typical court was approached by a tunnel entrance with dwellings on three sides of the courtyard and the communal privies, ash pits, well or pump on the fourth side.

The quality of the working-class housing was variable, but the site of the archaeological excavations at the western end of Edgbaston Street lay on the fringes of one of the most notorious slum areas of Birmingham. This area stretched from Smallbrook

Typical Birmingham slum housing of the 19th century. One of many unsanitary courts, c.1875.

Street and Worcester Street, both adjoining Edgbaston Street, up to New Street. New Street Station now occupies the middle of this area and indeed its construction, between 1847 and 1854 (it was completely rebuilt in 1964-71, with a shopping centre on top), involved the demolition of what were amongst the worst of Birmingham's slums, in a damp but conveniently low-lying area called 'the Froggery'.

The likewise damp area along Smithfield Passage may not have been much better, and material dumped into the open sewer provides evidence of the variety of small-scale industrial processes, including leather working, metalworking, glass making, and button making carried out in the nearby workshops. Leather working is particularly well-represented (the proximity of the former Welch's Skin Yard will be remembered), with large quantities of leather off-cuts, mainly discarded scraps, being recovered. Metalworking is better represented at Park Street and will be discussed later in this chapter. The evidence for glass making is provided by the waste from glass blowing and several examples of ceramic crucibles, some stained with a green, vitreous fluid (there is documentary evidence for a glassworks nearby on Edgbaston Street, built 1777-78).

Button making

The evidence for button making is of particular interest. Button making – a part of the 'toy trade' – is virtually synonymous with Birmingham industry in the 18th and early 19th century (by the middle of the 19th century the industry, while still a major employer, was in decline). While the typical 'Brummagem button' was of gilt metal, a variety of materials was used, including cloth, silk and linen buttons stretched over a metal frame, together with jet, glass, bone, horn, box wood, rubber and leather. Typical too is factory production – symbolised by Matthew Boulton's manufactory at Soho – where each button would pass through numerous hands and several mechanical devices to achieve the finished product. But

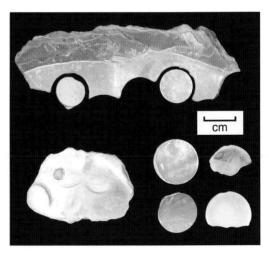

Mother-of-pearl button-making debris from the ditch at Edgbaston Street, early 19th century. At the top is a piece of shell from which button blanks have been cut. Bottom left is a piece of shell with preliminary incisions for the making of button blanks. Bottom right are examples of button blanks.

factory production is only part of the story, although twice as many men, women and children were employed in this mechanised aspect of the industry than in more small-scale, craft production.

Amongst the material dumped into the ditch behind Edgbaston Street was debris from the manufacture of mother-of-pearl buttons, including six button 'blanks' and two fragments of mother of pearl, one with holes where the button blanks had been removed and one scored for the removal of button blanks. Also found were numerous oyster shells, which were probably intended for button manufacture.

The making of mother-of-pearl buttons was a Birmingham speciality and by 1866 the industry employed around 2,000 people. Vast quantities of shells were imported from the East Indies, the Philippines, the Red Sea and the Persian Gulf. However, it was the only branch of the button trade not to have been extensively mechanised by the middle of the century. This was because, due to the fragility of the material, it had to be turned on a foot lathe. So the buttons were generally manufactured by 'garret-masters' operating from their own small premises. One such small workshop must have been situated to the rear of Edgbaston Street.

There were three main stages in the production of a mother-of-pearl button. First the blanks were cut from the shell using a tubular saw. Second, the blank was drilled through to create the holes or it was fitted with a shank and split pin. Finally – the most skilled part of the process – the button was engraved or faceted, and then polished.

The making of mother-of-pearl buttons declined in the later part of the 19th century, in part due to the introduction of cheaper buttons made from corozo nuts, a form of vegetable ivory from Venezuela. At the beginning of the 20th century shell buttons were replaced by plastic ones.

Park Street

We will move directly from Edgbaston Street to Park Street to continue our investigation of the archaeological evidence for Birmingham's transformation during the 17th and 18th centuries. We have skipped the second piece of our jigsaw puzzle, Moor Street, for the simple reason that virtually no evidence of this period – just one heavily-truncated pit – had survived. We need read no more into this than that the intensity of later building on the site, in the 19th and 20th centuries, had obliterated the remains. However, the single pit and all the medieval remains had been sealed by a 'dark earth' similar to that identified at Edgbaston Street.

At the Park Street site, however, there were extensive – and, in some cases, very well preserved – remains belonging to this crucial period of Birmingham's history.

The majority of the remains consisted of a mass of pits of different shapes and sizes. The pits themselves – there were more than fifty of them – and the remains within them are testimony to intensive industrial activity of various types being

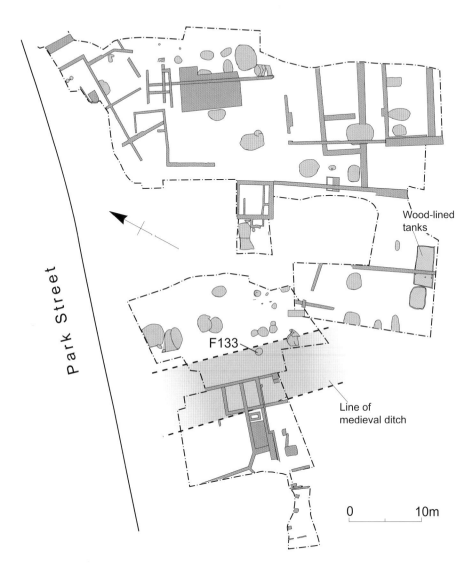

The Park Street site in the 17th and 18th centuries contained more than fifty pits, many filled with industrial debris, and two wood-lined tanks.

carried out in the 'back plot' area to the rear of Park Street. The pits contained, variously, slag (often in large quantities), hammerscale, fragments of crucibles, ash, clinker, charcoal, pottery, brick, tile, fragments of clay pipes, animal bones, worked animal bones, glass, iron nails and a range of iron and copper alloy objects. Some of the pits also contained the charred or waterlogged remains of plants, and in selected cases samples were taken of the soil containing these remains for specialist analysis.

The science of rubbish

All in all, a huge quantity of material – mostly discarded waste or rubbish really – was recovered from the excavation of the pits at Park Street. Back at the University, the task facing the archaeologists was to try and make sense of it all. Experts from the University and further afield undertook the painstaking specialist analysis of the different categories of material from the pits. Specialist reports (parts of much longer studies of all the material from the Bull Ring excavations) were prepared on the metal-working debris, the pottery, the animal bones, the plant remains, the clay tobacco pipes and the wide range of miscellaneous 'small finds'.

The 'science of rubbish' – some of the glass finds from the Park Street site. Two 18th-century wine bottles, and a medicine bottle, ink well, wine glass and water bottle of 19th-century date.

The analyses carried out and the information collected enabled several questions to be addressed. What activities had been carried out on the site and in the vicinity? Were there any differences between the activities carried out in different parts of the site? Did the nature of the activities change through time? Can we infer anything about the status (middle or working class) of those living and working at the site? Trying to answer such questions from the discarded debris found in pits is the 'science of rubbish', as archaeology is sometimes called. To illustrate how it works let's take a look at just one of the fifty plus pits relating to the 17th-18th-century phase of activity at Park Street and see what we can learn from it. Then we will look at the general picture which has emerged from the study of all the pits and their contents.

History from a pit

The pit we have selected to have a close look at was labelled F133, meaning 'feature number 133' of the Park Street excavations. It was a pretty ordinary circular pit – not especially large – measuring 1.3m in diameter and with a maximum depth of 1.05m.

The upper fill of the pit (soil layer 1125) contained large quantities of slag, bottle glass, pottery, clay tobacco pipe, tile and animal bone, together with many fragments of crucible, a brass buckle and 29 faceted glass stones. What does all this tell us? Let's start with the date of the pit. The large group of pottery from the pit suggested to the specialist, Stephanie Rátkai, a date in the range 1725-1750, with nothing later than 1750. The clay pipes told a slightly different story as they were of a type generally assigned to the range 1760-1800. So the pottery suggested the first half of the 18th century and the clay pipes suggested the second half of the

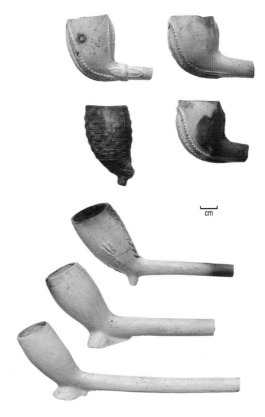

Clay tobacco pipes of the 18th and 19th centuries from the Park Street excavations.

18th century. How should we explain this apparent contradiction? Well, a lot of people look after their pottery; on my mother's shelves are crockery sets which the family had when I was a child – they are at least 40 years old. On the other hand, clay tobacco pipes – the 'cigarettes' of their day – were not kept for long, only days or weeks. So the pottery may have been a decade or two old when it was discarded, but it is unlikely that the pit was filled in as late as 1800 because you would expect at least one or two pieces of pottery later than 1750 if this was the case. So a date around 1760 seems about right. The other finds did not help with the dating much – the bottle glass looked 17th century but was perhaps later; the buckle was 18th century.

Having established the date of the pit (or rather the date it was filled in) – around 1760 – let's take a look at what its contents can tell us about what was going on in its vicinity. The most striking aspect of the contents of the pit was the large amount of metal-working debris that it contained. The fill of the pit contained no less than four kilograms of slag, the debris from metal working. The bulk of this material, just under three kilograms, was 'non-diagnostic' which, as the classification suggests, means that it cannot, on visual inspection, be assigned to any specific metallurgical process. However, 763 grams consisted of 'hearth bottoms' from iron smithing. Hearth bottoms, as we saw in an earlier chapter, are the bowl-shaped lumps of slag that accumulate in the bottom of a smith's hearth. Smithing is the hot working of iron and is not to be confused with smelting, the extraction of iron from the ore. There is no evidence of smelting at Park Street or the other Bull Ring sites at any period; the iron was imported to the site, probably from the Black Country. The hearth bottoms contained lumps of coal, which was evidently the fuel used by the Park Street iron smiths.

We have encountered evidence of iron smithing earlier at Park Street, in the 15th and 16th centuries, but a new feature in the 18th century is evidence for the working of other metals. Of the slag in our pit, 320 grams could be identified as slag arising from the melting of copper alloy and when the specialist, Matthew Nicholas, analysed it using a method known as X-ray fluorescence, the analysis showed the presence of copper and zinc, the ingredients of brass.

Interesting though the evidence from the slag is, more impressive is what could be learned from the large number of crucible fragments found in the pit. There were no less than 43 broken pieces of crucible in the fill of the pit. The crucibles from Park Street were flat-based pottery vessels, generally about 12cm in diameter, with thick walls and near vertical sides. They had spent a long time at high temperatures; in most cases the intense heat had caused the outer layer of crucible to begin to change to a glassy or vitreous state. These 'vitrified layers' contained metallic droplets, mostly microscopic in size, which could be analysed to determine what metals had been melted in the crucibles.

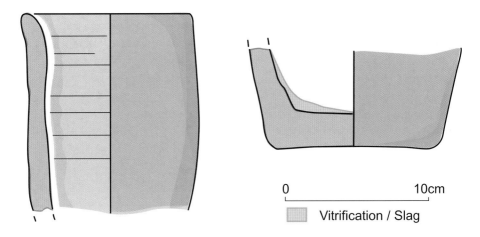

Sketches of typical crucibles from the Park Street site.

Seven of the crucibles from the pit were selected by Matthew Nicholas for detailed analysis in the laboratory. Samples were cut with a rock saw and mounted for analysis under a scanning electron microscope. The compositions of crucibles, vitrified layers and metal droplets were determined using a device called an 'energy dispersive spectrometer' attached to the microscope. The majority of the crucibles had been used to melt brass, an alloy of copper and zinc. However, one of the crucibles contained gunmetal, an alloy of copper that includes both zinc and tin. Very detailed analysis of another crucible revealed that the inner vitrified surface contained a very high amount of soda, suggesting that crushed glass was perhaps being used as a flux.

So, our pit has so far revealed that sometime around (probably before) 1760, iron working and the melting of brass and gunmetal was being carried out in the vicinity. What was being made? 'Toys', most likely, in the sense of small metal items like buttons and buckles. As chance would have it, our pit even produced a broken fragment of a copper alloy (probably brass) buckle of 18th-century date.

Buckles were big business in 18th-century Birmingham. The making of buckles 'for hats, breeches, or shoe' was the foremost of the toy trades and Birmingham was one of the largest suppliers in the country with an export trade to match. However, fashion is fickle and as our 18th-century friend William Hutton wrote 'the fashion of today is thrown into the casting pot to-morrow'. It was the introduction of shoelaces around 1790 that killed the buckle trade. The buckle manufacturers railed against the 'effeminate shoe string' or the 'slovenly ribbon', but to no avail. In 1791 the manufacturers even petitioned the Prince of Wales to help the 'more than 20,000 persons who in consequence of the prevalence of shoe strings and slippers' were unemployed or experiencing great hardship. The Prince ordered his followers to wear buckles instead of shoe strings, but fashion is an unforgiving master and even such royal sympathy was no use. By 1800 the making of buckles had almost ceased; thankfully, people still needed buttons.

Our pit has still more to tell us. A soil sample was taken from the pit for analysis of the plant remains present. What Marina Ciaraldi found was remarkably more varied than the range of plants she had found in the medieval samples. There was the usual range of weeds, of course, and a large quantity of hemp, indicating that hemp-working and textile preparation were still important in this period (we will come back to this later). There was also turnip and

Copper-alloy objects found on the Park Street excavations. They are of a range of dates. 1- Button inlaid with pale blue-green glass; 2 – Ornamental fitting; 3 – Part of buckle or clothing hook; 4 – Hooped earring; 5 & 6 – Pins; 7 – Thimble.

beet, suggesting vegetable gardens, but rose too, suggesting an ornamental garden. Then there was a range of fruits – plums, strawberry, fig and grape – and hazelnut. There was even hop, an ingredient in beer making (remember how the house on Edgbaston Street described in an advert of 1765 had a 'brewhouse with a pump').

This wide variety of plant remains not only reflects a more extensive and diverse trade in fruit and vegetables, but suggests high living in the vicinity – figs, grapes and roses, not the sort of thing you associate with workmen. This raises the question of the different use of space in the Park Street plots – were there grand town houses on the street frontage and workshops to the rear?

We could pursue this question and others by looking more closely at the pottery from the pit. What was it used for – storage, cooking or tableware? What was the likely social status of its users? More questions to be tackled by 'the science of rubbish'. However, we can better tackle these questions by looking at the pattern that emerges from the study of the fifty or more pits of this period on the Park Street site taken together. The archaeologists had to work through the evidence from each pit in turn (although not all were as rich as Pit F133) but we can just look at the general picture that emerges, along with the occasional surprise.

Life and work on Park Street

When Stephanie Rátkai examined all the pottery from the 17th- and 18th-century pits at Park Street she found that they fell into distinct chronological groups. No occupation of this period was found to the west of the old boundary ditch that marked the rear boundary of the plots fronting onto Digbeth, although the ditch itself, having fallen into disuse since perhaps the 14th century, seems to have been dug out again around the beginning of the 17th century. Thus all the remains uncovered during the excavations belonged to plots fronting onto Park Street. Any remains of the 17th and 18th centuries in the rear end of plot fronting onto Digbeth had no doubt been destroyed by the intensive building activity that took place here in the 19th century.

A few small groups of pits dated to the 17th century. However, in the period covering the late 17th century to the mid 18th century the intensity of activity on the site seems to have increased, to judge from the number of pits assigned to this period. Also the focus of activity seems to have moved back somewhat from the frontage, so the pits of this period form a rough band running from east to west across the site. A further change is an apparent intensification of industrial activity. Most of the pits producing crucible fragments belong to this group, and indeed the pit we looked at in detail – F133 – is an example of one of these. Several pits also had a distinctive 'bellying out' shape, suggesting they had once been lined, together with substantial quantities of ash, clinker and charcoal, and these pits may have had a particular industrial function.

One of the late 17th / early 18th-century pits, located slightly apart from the main cluster, contained a particularly interesting group of finds. Most noteworthy amongst its contents was a large quantity of worked bone,

Bone working in the 17th and early 18th centuries at Park Street. Above, a range of handles in various stages of completion. Below, a collection of bone off-cuts from a single pit. The pit also contained a large collection of hammerscale from iron working. Is this evidence of knife manufacture?

mostly sawn off-cuts from sheep bones. The appearance of the bone waste was consistent with the manufacture of knife handles. However, the pit also contained slag, hearth bottoms and a large quantity of hammerscale, all waste from ironworking (hammerscale is the debris from hammering hot iron). Knife hafting and smithing were normally two distinct occupations, but can we see here the debris from a cutler's workshop, where complete knives were made as part of one business?

Two large rectangular pits, or rather tanks, were of a very different character to all the other pits and clearly served a distinct industrial function. The two tanks stood side by side at the southern limit of the site, on the line of the medieval boundary ditch which had defined the back end of the Park Street burgage plots. The larger of the two tanks, measuring about 4m by 2m, had been lined with wooden planking kept in place by upright posts; the damp conditions had preserved much of this timber lining intact. The smaller tank measured about 3m by 2m. It also had vertical sides and a flat bottom, and around the edges of the base of the tank

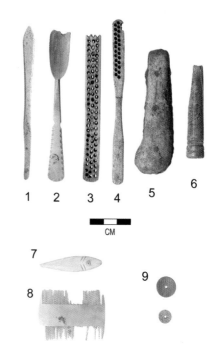

Bone artefacts from the Park Street excavations, mainly 17th and 18th century in date. 1 – Spatula; 2 – Spoon; 3 – Brush; 4 – Tooth brush?; 5 – Knife handle; 6 – Handle?; 7 – Gaming token?; 8 – Nit comb; 9 – Buttons. Note that the possible tooth brush is unfinished – it broke during manufacture when the third row of holes was being drilled.

was a series of postholes shaped to take pointed timber uprights which would have held in place the lining planks. A wicker canopy had collapsed (or been thrown) into the pit and survived in a well-preserved state. More remarkable was the fact that the wicker canopy lay on top of an almost complete wooden chair of mid 17th-century date; the chair had obviously been disposed of after the tank had fallen into disuse. The chair, probably of oak, was of a heavy, solid style with turned, 'barley-twist' decoration on the front legs; fragments of the leather seat and back and of the organic stuffing survived.

Despite their good preservation, there is a lack of direct evidence for the function of these two tanks, although they were clearly water tanks and served an industrial function. Given the evidence for textile preparation on the site in the

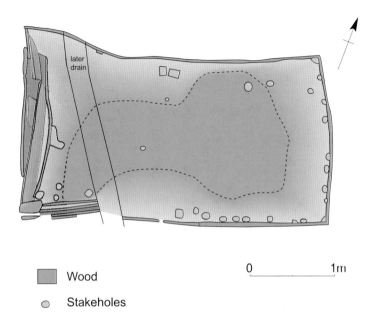

Wood

Stakeholes

0   1m

A plan of the large wood-lined tank at Park Street. The holes for the stakes which held the planking in place can be seen around the edge of the pit.

Excavating the wood-lined tanks at the Park Street site. Just in front of the archaeologist at the bottom of the photo can be seen the blackened timbers lining one end of the large tank.

90

An almost intact 17th-century chair comes to light in the infilling of the smaller of the two wood-lined tanks.

preceding centuries, possibly hemp and flax retting, and the persistence of hemp in the botanical samples from the 17th and 18th centuries, an association with textile manufacture seems most likely; dyeing is a possibility.

Even if we cannot be sure what the water tanks were used for, the archaeological dig at Park Street has provided evidence for a diverse range of industries in the 17th and 18th centuries: textile processing (probably), iron smithing, brass working and bone working.

Let's now take a closer look at the pottery to see if we can work out from that a bit more about what was going on on the site, and of the lifestyle of its occupants and their social status. A good place to start is with the large collection of pottery that was found in the infilling of the two timber-lined tanks. The large size of the pottery sherds, the small amount of pottery from earlier phases of the occupation of the site, and the fact that pottery sherds from different layers within the infilling of tanks could be fitted together, all indicated that this large group of pottery was dumped into the tanks in a single episode. Detailed analysis of the group suggested that the greater part of the pottery was more or less contemporary and dated to the late 1770s or early 1780s. The pottery was probably dumped in the pit a few years after this, in what looks very much like a house clearance. If the mid 17th-century chair was dumped into one of the disused tanks at the same time it was already more than a century old; an unwanted, possibly broken, and out-of-fashion chair that had perhaps long been sitting in a cellar or suchlike.

In order to study this large and important collection of pottery, Stephanie Rátkai called in assistance from David Barker of the Potteries Museum, Stoke-on-Trent. David is an expert in the pottery of this period, and indeed much of the collection had probably been manufactured in Stoke.

The collection of pottery could be divided into two broad groups, so-called 'refined wares' on the one hand, and coarsewares and other more utilitarian vessels on the other hand. The refined wares are what the name suggests, they are at the posher end of the spectrum, and were dominated by three main 18th-century pottery types – creamware, white salt-glazed stoneware and brown salt-glazed stoneware. The type of vessels made of refined wares are tablewares, tea wares and other drinking vessels. The tablewares include such things as creamware plates with

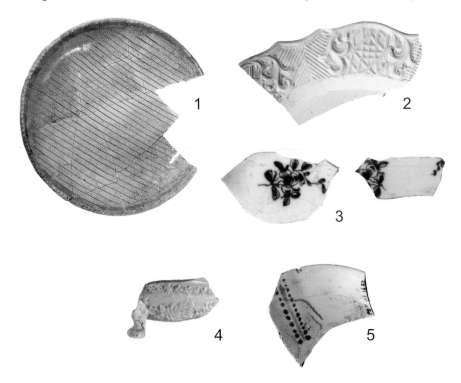

A selection of the pottery dumped into the two disused wood-lined tanks around 1790, and possibly representing a house clearance. 1 – Dish, trailed/feathered slipware, early 18th century; 2 – Plate, salt-glazed stoneware, c. 1720-60; 3 – Saucer, soft paste porcelain,; 4 – Teapot?, lion's mask and paw foot, moulded salt glaze ware; 5 – Saucer, decorated creamware, c. 1750-1770.

'royal', 'queen's', feather scalloped and *fleurs de lys* edges. There is also a lobed salad dish. Tea wares include teabowls and saucers, a milk jug and part of what is probably a teapot, in white salt-glazed stoneware with moulded vine decoration and lion's mask and paw feet. Other refined ware vessels include a range of mugs, jugs and a chamber pot.

The refined wares reflect the growing popularity and availability of ceramics in the years after about 1760, replacing vessels of pewter, wood and horn that were popular in earlier periods. The most famous producer was Josiah Wedgwood (1730-95), whose promotion of his own creamware, marketed as 'Queensware', brought these products into the homes of the gentry and middle classes in an unprecedented way. Most, if not all, the refined wares from Park Street were probably manufactured in north Staffordshire.

The refined wares speak of refined behaviour 'upstairs', drinking tea in the parlour, perhaps, whilst having polite conversation about the new fashion for shoe strings and the appalling impact it is having on the town's buckle manufacturers. The remainder of the pottery tells a more 'below stairs' story, with a range of kitchenwares and more utilitarian tablewares. The kitchenwares comprise such things as coarseware bowls, storage jars and a strainer. The utilitarian tablewares include platters, dishes, mugs and tankards.

Taken as a whole, the collection of pottery dumped in the tanks represents both the 'upstairs' and 'below stairs' ceramic components of a middle-class household that were discarded together perhaps around 1790. The nearest place for the house to have stood would have been on the Park Street frontage. Does this collection represent a house clearance? Could it be associated with a 'flight of the middle classes' from areas such as Park Street (and, as we saw earlier, Edgbaston Street) around the end of the 18th century? What has this to do with the so-called 'dark earth' which was found at Park Street as well as Moor Street and Edgbaston Street?

These are questions that we will tackle in a moment, but first we shall take a brief look at the range of pottery associated with the numerous other pits to the rear of the Park Street frontage. We have envisioned a fine Georgian house on the frontage and we have examined the pottery from such a house, but what can the pottery associated with the industrial debris of (mainly) metalworking tell us?

With the exception of two pits (one of which was quite likely filled in in the same dumping episode as the two tanks), refined wares are strikingly absent. Although there is likely to be a chronological aspect to this (many of the pits date to the period before such refined wares came into fashion), it suggests that the pottery found in these pits came from a different source. What we find in the pits is a range of kitchenwares, such as bowls and jars, and unrefined 'tablewares', such as dishes, mugs and tankards. These may have been used by the workers themselves, who were probably small-scale independent or semi-independent craftsmen. The hours were long and a smith's forge is as good a place as any to knock up a quick meal, and furthermore smithing is hot, thirsty work so we can imagine the mugs being used to consume copious quantities of light beers and ale. Be that as it may, functional analysis of the pottery from Park Street conjures up a typical 18th-century pattern of combining middle-class domestic occupation (usually to the front of the plot) with industrial workshops (usually to the rear).

The Birmingham 'dark earth' revisited

This pattern was set to change. When Bob Burrows and his team of archaeologists were in the early stages of excavating the site they found a dark earth layer extending across the entire area of the excavation, ranging from 0.2 to 0.7m in depth. It overlay all the pits that we have been describing and clearly marks a radical change, or series of changes, in the organisation and use of the site. It was followed by a range of industrial buildings of 19th-century date. Of necessity, the layer was removed by mechanical excavator in order to get down to the archaeological remains beneath it, and just three 1m-square sample areas of it were dug by hand. This limited both understanding of the layer and the amount of pottery and other material that was recovered from it. Nevertheless, study of the pottery and other material from the 'dark earth' showed that it was not in fact a uniform deposit of a single origin and date. In some areas it may have been a 'cultivation soil' of early to mid-17th century date, similar to that uncovered at Edgbaston Street. Elsewhere it contained substantial quantities of brick and tile and looked more like a demolition layer. The layer overlying the two timber-lined tanks dated to the early 19th century, and so was a century later than the 'cultivation soil' at Edgbaston Street.

Thus the Birmingham 'dark earth', although such a prominent feature of the excavations at Edgbaston Street, Moor Street and Park Street, does not represent a uniform phenomenon. Rather, it seems to reflect a complex sequence of events spread over the 18th century, which witness the final decisive stages of Birmingham's transformation from what was still in the 17th century essentially a medieval market town to the industrial giant of the 19th century.

Insofar as this transformation is manifest in the results of the excavations at Edgbaston Street and Park Street, first we witness the intensification and diversification of essentially 'medieval' industries such as leather working, textile working and metalworking in the late 17th and early 18th centuries (the 'fuse', to return to an analogy we used at the beginning of this chapter). Then, in the middle years of the 18th century, we see our first phase of major change (the 'detonator bomb'), marked by a hiatus in these industries in the traditional mode, represented by the 'cultivation soils', and by 'gentrification', symbolised by middle-class residences on the frontages. Finally, in the late 18th century and early 19th century, we witness the social downgrading of both areas, represented by possible 'house clearance' dumps and the later demolition deposits at Park Street, followed by extensive rebuilding in a predominantly industrial mode (the 'explosion').

Of course, this is a tentative and overly simplified scheme, with much of the action happening 'off stage', but the Bull Ring excavations set an agenda for the future archaeological exploration of the key transformative period in Birmingham's history. Such archaeological exploration offers us the potential not only of new forms of tangible and sometimes intimate evidence, but also a new perspective on the 'town of a thousand trades'. The insights – and intimate detail – of the archaeological perspective are nowhere better demonstrated than in the results of the excavation of St. Martin's churchyard, which forms the main subject of the concluding chapters of this book.

Chapter 7

St. Martin's and its Churchyard

Jo Adams with Simon Buteux

So far in this book we have charted the history of Birmingham through the results from three excavations carried out in advance of the construction of the new Bullring complex – Edgbaston Street, Moor Street and Park Street. These excavations have carried the story of Birmingham up to the opening years of the 19th century. In this chapter and those following we change tack and pursue the story from a new perspective, not the archaeology of the living but the archaeology of the dead, those buried in St. Martin's churchyard.

The excavation of St. Martin's churchyard, carried out in 2001, arose from the need to lower the level of the churchyard for the creation of St. Martin's Square as part of the overall Bullring development. This entailed the archaeological excavation of 857 burials, the majority of 19th-century date. The full or partial excavation of churchyards in advance of development is by no means unusual – at St. Martin's partial excavation has taken place several times in the past, most notably in advance of the rebuilding and extending of the church in 1872, in advance of the building of the church hall and vestry in 1953, and in the 1960s to facilitate the widening of roads associated with the Bull Ring Centre. In each case the work was carried out with sensitivity and the human remains affected were reburied, either elsewhere in the churchyard or in another appropriate cemetery.

The principal difference in the case of the 2001 excavations was that the archaeological and scientific significance of the burials was by this time appreciated and, under strict guidance from the relevant authorities, the work was carried out by archaeologists from the University of Birmingham, with an opportunity being given for scientific study of the remains prior to reburial. In accordance with Home Office and Diocesan directions, advance notices of the archaeological work were given. This was to allow any surviving relatives to come forward and enable the removal of members of their family from St. Martin's and reburial at a preferred churchyard or cemetery. In the event, no surviving relatives came forward.

As we shall see, the burials uncovered in St. Martin's churchyard fell into two groups, a small group where the names of those buried could be identified and a much larger group where they could not. All the named remains were reburied in St. Martin's whilst those who could not be identified were reburied at Quinton Cemetery. A memorial service, attended by representatives of those involved in the

St. Martin's and its churchyard in the 1960s. The Bull Ring Centre and markets are in the foreground.

excavations, was held on Tuesday 10th June 2003. Some of the burials excavated were accompanied by personal items, for example rings and hair accessories; following study these were reburied with the individuals concerned.

The archaeology of the dead

It will be clear from what has just been said that the archaeology of the dead is a different sort of archaeology to the archaeology of the living. Archaeologists are acutely aware of this fact, and in this context it is no longer appropriate to describe archaeology as the 'science of rubbish'. Instead, burial archaeology affords us privileged access to the remains of the people of Birmingham themselves. The work must be carried out with respect. Each skeleton is much more than an object, it is the mortal remains of somebody who was loved by family and friends, and who was usually buried in the hope – however vaguely formulated – that their soul would rise up to heaven to begin a new life.

However, it is a simple fact of death that a body buried in a churchyard will not usually remain undisturbed for long. We can appreciate this by viewing the gravestones in the churchyard of any medieval church. The churchyard may be full and many graves are marked by headstones of the 20th, 19th and perhaps 18th centuries, but often few that are earlier than this. In part this is because the practice of marking the grave of each individual with a gravestone is of relatively recent origin, but in part it is because the intensive use of the burial ground for the burial of the dead from a whole parish over perhaps nine centuries has meant that the earlier burials have been disturbed and the bones dispersed. One way of appreciating this rather grim fact is to look at the height of the graveyard itself. The ground is sometimes much higher than the foundations of the church and the ground surrounding the churchyard – it is centuries of burial that has caused this. In the case of the churchyard of St. Martin's, which was not designed to deal with the dead from a vastly inflated urban population, the problem was extreme. Nineteenth-century illustrations show the churchyard wall towering above the surrounding streets and William Hutton, with a typical apposite turn of phrase, wrote 'the dead are raised up, and instead of the church burying the dead, the dead would in time, have buried the church'.

Thus it is was that the burials surviving in St. Martin's churchyard at the time of its archaeological excavation in 2001 were predominantly late 18th century and 19th century in date (only a handful of burials took place in St. Martin's churchyard after 1863). Burial archaeology offers a number of fascinating perspectives on the past. First, we can learn something of the burial rituals and attitudes to the dead. Such rituals and attitudes are not static but hold up a mirror both to differences between the social classes and to changing social values. For example, lavish funerals could not only mark grief and respect for the dead person but were also a means for living relatives to show

St. Martin's churchyard during archaeological excavation in 2001, with the Rotunda in the background.

off their wealth and status, and values changed with respect to how elaborate funerals were to be and how much money should be spent on them. In Chapter 8 we will survey the variety of types of burial found in St. Martin's churchyard. Second, we can learn about the funerary trade itself. Undertaking was not an insignificant profession but one with real economic impact; people – sometimes vulnerable, grief-stricken people – were prepared to part with large sums of money. From archaeology we learn particularly about the material side of the profession – the burial garments, the coffins and the tombs. Indeed, the manufacture of metal fittings for coffins was no small part of Birmingham's 'toy trade'. This aspect of the archaeology of St. Martin's churchyard will be explored in Chapter 9. Third, from the scientific study of the skeletons of the dead themselves we can learn something of their lives (often tragically short) and of the illnesses they suffered, together with the demographics of the population. This is particularly interesting for Birmingham in the late 18th and early 19th centuries because this was, as we saw in the last chapter, a period of massive population growth with all the attendant health problems of crowded urban living in often unsanitary conditions. A summary of the preliminary results of this scientific research, carried out by Dr Megan Brickley, Dr Helena Berry and Gaynor Western, is given in Chapter 10.

However, burial archaeology is perhaps at its most fascinating when, from inscriptions on coffin plates, we know the names of the dead and can trace something of their lives from documentary sources. Then the different perspectives can be combined to form a rounded picture of the lives and deaths of ordinary Birmingham people – little biographies that cast a particular light on life in 19th-century Birmingham. It is true, as we shall see, that these 'ordinary people' are almost exclusively from the middle classes because it was only in the more expensive burial vaults that the coffins and coffin plates – providing the names of the dead – tended to survive reasonably intact. Nevertheless, these short biographies, which form the subject of the final chapter of the book, provide an insight into the lives of the sort of people who made Birmingham into 'the first manufacturing town in the world'.

Before beginning our exploration of the archaeology of St Martin's churchyard in the next chapter we should provide some background on the later history of the church and of its churchyard.

St. Martin's-in-the-Bull Ring

The early church of St. Martin's that stood in the 12th-century market place would have been a simple Norman affair. In the late 13th century it was completely rebuilt in the fashionable Decorated style, an indication of the prosperity of Birmingham by this time. This medieval church survived, through numerous vicissitudes, until the late 19th century.

The medieval church was built in red sandstone which weathered badly, requiring frequent repairs and alterations. Finally, in 1690, it was deemed necessary to encase the whole in brick. While the elements put pressure on St. Martin's from the outside, Birmingham's growing population put pressure on the church from the inside. In the 1730s substantial alterations were made to the interior of St. Martin's in an attempt to accommodate the growing congregation, with new galleries inserted. In the words of William Hutton again 'every recess capable of only admitting the body of an infant, was converted into a seat'.

St. Martin's Church in 1835. Due to decay of the sandstone the nave was encased in brick in 1690.

St. Martin's Church in 1875, shortly after rebuilding in the Gothic style.

Such overcrowding was not a problem if you could afford to pay for a good pew. From the late 17th century pews could be bought or rented. This is illustrated by an advertisement of 1812 in the local paper:

> *'St. Martin's Church – To be let (on lease, if desired) the most distinguished Pew in this Church, late in the occupation of S.T. Galton Esq., in front of the gallery directly opposite the Pulpit.'*

As the next chapter will show, the divisions amongst the living between those who could afford their own protected space in the church and those who could not is almost perfectly reflected in the graveyard in the divisions amongst the dead.

After various repairs – the spire was an ongoing problem – and an abortive plan for complete rebuilding in 1849 (only £5,000 of the necessary £12,000 could be raised by public appeal), St. Martin's was eventually rebuilt in 1872. All the buildings, except for the tower and spire, were demolished and a new church, 50ft longer than the old one, was built in the Gothic style.

The new church was damaged during the Second World War by a bomb which landed outside the west door in 1941, but was restored after the war in 1947. A new church hall and vestry were added to the south side of the church in 1953, with a further extension in 2003, resulting in the building as it is today.

The churchyard

The churchyard of St. Martin's has suffered as many vicissitudes – if not more – as the church itself. It has been affected not only by the various rebuildings, alterations and extensions of the church, but also by the redevelopment of the congested market area around it, which has led to repeated modifications of the churchyard boundary. Further, like the church itself but to an even greater extent, the churchyard suffered from having to cope with a population grown out of all proportion to that for which it was intended.

The church burial records begin in 1556 and initially the number of burials was modest enough, averaging about two hundred a year. However, by the 18th century, when Birmingham's population began to take off, the problems were already severe. We have seen how the churchyard grew so much in height such that Hutton feared the dead might bury the church. Rather more prosaically, a report on the churchyard of 1781 declared that:

'the ancient walls thereof on the south side and south east sides had in several parts bulged and given way and became dangerous to such as passed along a certain street or land adjoining the said churchyard.'

This was work for the Street Commissioners, whose activities in cleaning up the market place and creating new market facilities were described in the previous chapter. So, under the auspices of the Act for Lightening and Cleansing the Streets, it became necessary to:

St. Martin's Lane in 1840. The churchyard wall can be seen on the extreme right. A massive retaining wall was needed due to the accumulation of centuries of burials in the churchyard.

'take down and rebuild the Ancient Wall with the Buttresses or supporters thereof and to strengthen the said wall by widening the same and make it substantial and durable...three feet and six inches or thereabouts in breadth.'

Nevertheless, the pressure continued relentlessly and in 1807 two-and-a-half acres of land were purchased in Park Street to form a detached burial ground for St. Martin's. Then, in 1810, a faculty was obtained to enlarge the churchyard itself by the purchase of land in Spiceal Street that was 'abutting on the part thereof to St. Martin's Churchyard'.

In 1851 and 1852 the number of burials in the churchyard reached a peak, when there were 2,900 and 3,252 respectively. This was not sustainable – something more radical needed to be done. It was not just the physical bulk of all these burials that was a problem, but the presence of so much rotting flesh and the disturbance of so many bones was not only a gruesome affront to decency but a public health hazard.

Such problems were by no means unique to St. Martin's, and the principal solution was the establishment of out-of-town cemeteries. As early as 1836 a group of nonconformists established the General Cemetery at Key Hill (it houses several

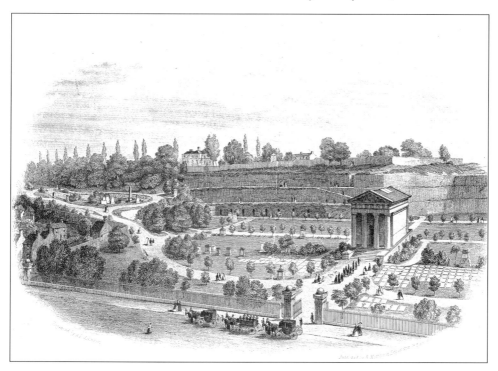

Warstone Lane cemetery, opened in 1848, was one of the earlier 'out of town' cemeteries established to relieve pressure on the town's churchyards.

of Birmingham's Victorian 'greats', including Joseph Chamberlain) and in 1848 an Anglican cemetery was established at nearby Warstone Lane. However, the Warstone Lane cemetery was a private venture and was available only for those who could afford it. In 1863 Birmingham's first public cemetery was opened by the Corporation on 105 acres of ground at Witton. The opening of Witton Cemetery corresponded with a near cessation of burial at St. Martin's: in 1863 there were 544 burials, in contrast to a total of 52 for the whole of the following period up to 1915, when the last burial took place.

Hand in hand with the policy of establishing new cemeteries went that of controlling burial in the old churchyards to limit the risk to public health. In 1873 the Secretary of State issued an Order in Council stating that all burials should be discontinued at churches throughout Birmingham, except in vaults and walled graves with an air-tight coffin. The unused burial grounds could be turned into parks, as happened at the Park Street burial ground (the detached burial ground of St. Martin's), which was transformed into Park Street Gardens and opened to the public in 1880. Around the same time St. Martin's churchyard was landscaped, with trees planted, turf laid and the surrounding iron railings renovated. This followed on from the rebuilding of the enlarged church in 1872, which had necessarily involved removal and disturbance of burials. In 1927 the City Council passed a bye law stating that all the closed burial grounds in the city, including St. Martin's, would become open to the public.

The final changes to St. Martin's churchyard, prior to the archaeological excavations of 2001 and subsequent landscaping, were related to the post-war redevelopment of the Bull Ring area in the 1950s and 1960s. In 1953 burials were removed from the south side of the church to accommodate the construction of the new church hall and vestry, and in the 1960s many monuments and remains were removed to Witton Cemetery to facilitate the new layout and widening of roads associated with the Bull Ring Centre. The combined effect of this was that all the churchyard to the south of the church was removed.

Despite its many vicissitudes St. Martin's church remains the most enduring symbol of Birmingham's past. The results of the excavation of its churchyard have opened a new and unexpected window onto that past.

Chapter 8

Graves and Tombs:
the Archaeology of St. Martin's Churchyard

Richard Cherrington with Simon Buteux

The documented history of St. Martin's churchyard gave the archaeologists some idea of what to expect below ground. However in the churchyard itself, with one exception, none of the funerary monuments and gravestones that had once stood above the graves survived in position. These monuments had formed the principal focus for mourning and remembrance but had been cleared away in the various phases of landscaping of the churchyard that had taken place since the church was rebuilt in 1872. Old photographs show what some of these monuments looked like. Many of the most impressive were 'chest tombs' and, as the name suggests, were

Excavated earth-cut graves, brick-lined graves and vaults in the churchyard. The empty area in the northwest corner of the churchyard is more apparent than real – landscaping work here did not require excavation down to the level of most of the graves.

shaped like a chest with slab top. Various gravestones were found lying flat on the surface or in the topsoil, often in a fragmentary state. Where the inscriptions on the gravestones could be read, they dated from the late 17th to the 19th century.

The absence of *in situ* burial monuments and gravestones deprived the archaeologists of the possibility of identifying the occupants of graves from the memorials above them. Only where coffin plates survived sufficiently well intact to be legible could the identity and/or date of burials be determined. With just one or two exceptions, such well-preserved coffin plates only survived in brick-lined graves and burial vaults; in the much more common simple, earth-cut graves such preservation was exceedingly rare. The vast majority of the burials in St. Martin's churchyard must, therefore, remain anonymous.

As we saw in the last chapter, much of the churchyard had been either built over by extensions to the church buildings or had been lost to road widening. The rebuilding of the church in 1872 to an extended plan had removed much of the eastern side of the churchyard, and the construction of the church hall and vestry in 1953 had removed the southern side of the churchyard. This meant that the archaeological excavations were confined to the northern and western sides of the churchyard. This is significant because in a church and its churchyard various locations are favoured for burial. The most prestigious location is within the church itself – this is where the early de Birmingham lords were buried (the recumbent stone effigies of three of them still survive). Outside the church the favoured location was the sunny southern and eastern sides of the church. The gloomy northern side of the churchyard, in the shadow of the church, was the least favoured location – here, the superstitious believed, the devil lurked in the shadows.

So the northern part of the churchyard, which was the focus of the excavations, was probably the last part to be used, when the more favourable locations had been filled up. Of course, with a graveyard that had to cope with such huge numbers as St. Martin's, few could afford to be choosy. Nevertheless, the location of the excavated portion of the graveyard has some implications for the date and status of the burials found there.

The date of the burials

A total of 857 burials were recorded during the excavations at St. Martin's. Evidence to date most of these burials was limited, but comprised such things as coffin fittings (or 'coffin furniture' as it is often called), personal items found with the deceased, and the stratigraphic relationships between the graves (many, as we shall see, were intercutting) and between the graves and dated burial vaults. From this it could be inferred that the vast majority of the burials dated to the first half of the 19th century, with only a handful of 18th-century date and later 19th-century date.

Excavation of the earliest dated burial in the churchyard. The copper alloy lettering on the coffin lid reads '172[?] [A]GE 85'.

The earliest dated burial, of the 1720s, was in an earth-cut grave and was identified from copper alloy lettering on the coffin lid reading [M?] [172?] [(A)GE] [85]. This was a good age by any standards – it is just possible that as a child the occupant of the grave had witnessed the sack of Birmingham by Prince Rupert in 1643! This grave, however, certainly did not represent the earliest burial in the northern part of the cemetery; it was cut into a charnel pit containing a jumble of poorly-preserved disarticulated human bones.

Few of the burials in simple earth-cut graves are likely to date much later than 1863, when, as we saw in the last chapter, records show that the number of burials in the churchyard declined steeply, and presumably none after 1873, when legislation was introduced banning burials except in vaults and walled graves. Burials in vaults continued, although in small numbers, up to 1915.

The resting place of the masses: earth-cut graves

The burials at St. Martin's comprised three main types. First, there were burials in a simple earth-cut grave. Second, there were burials in brick-lined graves with a barrel-vaulted or slab roof. Third, there were burials in brick-built family vaults. The first

A typical single burial in an earth-cut grave. Note, however, that in this case the top of the skull has been sawn off to perform an autopsy. Virtually all trace of the coffin has disappeared, as was generally the case with the earth-cut graves.

type – burial in an earth-cut grave – was by far the most common, accounting for 749 of the 857 burials recorded during the excavations, and will be discussed first.

The most common form of burial in an earth-cut grave was a single burial with the body lying on its back, head to the west (so the risen body would face Jerusalem), buried in a wooden coffin with metal fittings – the standard Christian mode of burial. The depths of the earth-cut graves were variable, and some appeared to be quite shallow, although it was usually impossible to determine the depth of burial accurately as the level of the contemporary ground surface was unknown. The state of preservation of the coffins and coffin furniture was likewise variable, ranging from quite well-preserved timber to barely visible stains.

Immediately to the north of the church the density of burials was very great, with many of the burials intercutting. When a later burial disturbed an earlier one the bones from the latter were gathered up by the grave diggers and put into a charnel-pit containing the jumbled remains of many other individuals. Several such charnel pits were excavated. Alternatively, the gravediggers would rebury disturbed remains in the backfill of the grave that had disturbed them. It is apparent that for many their grave was not so much a last resting place as a temporary residence.

Given the density of burials, the absence of formal records that showed where burials were and the fact that 'permanent' grave markers in stone (as opposed to wood) only became generally popular from the late 18th century (and then only for those who could afford them), it would have been difficult to find an empty spot for a new burial, or at least a spot that did not contain a relatively recent burial. The sexton (the church official in charge of burial) had several options. One traditional approach involved using different areas of the churchyard in rotation so that the chances of disturbing a recent burial were minimised. Another approach, which could be used in conjunction with rotation, was to probe the ground with a 'boring rod'. Nevertheless, the disturbance of recent burials – those where the body had not yet been reduced to a skeleton – did occur. A rather grisly example of this from St. Martin's was the finding of an isolated human arm with all the bones intact and in position – it must have been severed from the body while the ligaments, at least, were still attached.

Despite the distress it could cause, at St. Martin's and other urban churchyards it was a simple consequence of arithmetic that new burials would disturb old ones. Furthermore, by the middle of the 19th century the mushrooming population and the fashion for 'permanent' gravestones, which inhibited 'rotational' burial, led to a crisis in the burial of the dead. The solution to the crisis, as we saw in the last chapter, was the foundation of municipal cemeteries and the placing of restrictions on the use of the old churchyards.

While the typical earth-cut grave contained a single body, there were some variants. In several cases two or more burials were stacked one on top of the other in a single grave. Such multiple burials may reflect the pressure on space, or they may contain members of the same family. The two explanations are not exclusive – in an overcrowded churchyard such 'stacked' burials may have been the only way loved ones could be put to rest together. There was, however, one example of a double burial with two adults lying side by side in a shallow grave cut. Both had their arms crossed over their chests, suggesting they had been buried in funerary shrouds or tightly wrapped in winding sheets. The use of shrouds and winding sheets in the burials at St. Martin's was evident both from surviving fragments of material and the recovery of numerous fastening pins.

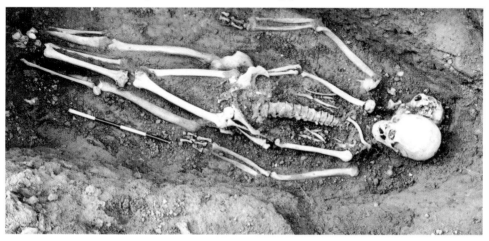

Two burials superimposed one on top of the other in a single grave.

Two burials side by side in a shallow grave cut. The folded arms suggest the bodies were tightly bound in winding sheets.

One of the most poignant aspects of the excavation of the churchyard was the number of infant burials uncovered. New-born babies and young infants were usually buried with only a winding sheet; in several cases babies were buried with their mother if both had died during childbirth. In some cases foetal remains were found within the womb area of female burials.

In keeping with Christian practice, very few of the burials included personal effects, although there were a few examples of wedding rings, jewellery and wig-curlers.

Status and security: brick-lined graves

One very clear aspect of 19th-century society was the distancing of the middle classes from the masses of the working classes. This was apparent in life in numerous ways, including the aspiration of the middle classes to remove themselves physically from the old parts of town with their slums and filth and out into the new suburbs such as Edgbaston. It was apparent too in the rental of exclusive pews within the church. As in life so in death. Scattered amongst the numerous earth-cut graves was a relatively small number of brick-lined graves; 23 were recorded during the excavation.

The brick-lined graves were not complex structures. The first task in their construction was to dig a straight-sided rectangular pit to receive the burial structure. This almost inevitably involved disturbing earth-cut graves. The pit was usually dug down to the natural sandstone, which was at a convenient depth of up to about 2.5m and required relatively little levelling in order to provide a sound footing for the brickwork. In other cases, courses of dry-laid or mortared bricks laid

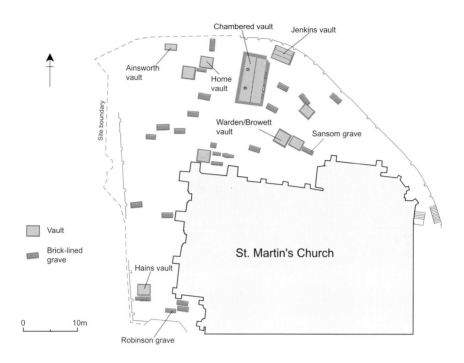

Excavated brick-lined graves and vaults in the churchyard. The graves and vaults of some identified individuals and families are indicated.

A barrel-roofed brick-lined grave.

A typical brick-lined grave roofed with a ledger stone.

flat formed the flooring. The brick-lined graves were roofed in two different ways, which were each equally common. One method was to provide the grave with a barrelled roof of brick. In this case the procedure was to first construct, from the inside of the pit, the two side walls, which would form the springer walls for the barrelled roof. Then wooden shuttering would be erected and the barrelled roof was built from the outside. Once the mortar had dried the end walls would have been built up from the inside, leaving an access trap. The second method was to roof the grave with a flat 'ledger' stone; sometimes an old gravestone was used for this purpose. It is possible that a barrel roof was the standard construction technique and that the use of ledger stones often occurred when the original roof was removed at a later date, perhaps for the insertion of additional burials.

Interior effects included whitewashing of the walls and incorporating 'putlog' holes to receive the timber coffin supports and serve as air vents (to allow gases to escape); alternatively putlogs were sometimes cut out of the existing brickwork. Iron fixtures associated with the coffin supports were also sometimes found.

The quality of the construction of the brick-lined graves was variable. The walls were made of either a single skin of bricks or a double skin; in several cases there was evidence that the former turned out not to be sufficiently stable. The majority were built of clamped red brick with a limed mortar, although machine-cut brick was also used. On inspection it was clear that a number of the structures incorporated a mixture of brick types of different periods; the builders were using recycled materials (this is also evident in the use of old gravestones as roofing slabs). Did the clients always know this was happening or were they being hoodwinked by the builder? The materials would probably have been the most expensive part of the job (labour was cheap and need not have been particularly skilled), many sins can be whitewashed, and is it likely that clients would have inspected the work closely? The 19th-century churchyard was a pretty gruesome place, as we have seen, and given the number of burials the activities of grave digging and tomb building must have been more or less continuous.

One of the brick-lined graves was of particularly shoddy construction. The side walls, of a single skin of brickwork, were so poorly constructed that two brick buttresses had to be built against the outside of each wall to prevent outward collapse; they had the opposite effect and the walls had started to collapse inwards. And, as the director of the excavations Richard Cherrington (who has worked as a builder as well as an archaeologist) puts it, the quality of the lime mortar was also 'questionable'. A further, rather comical, sign of 'cowboy' building was that although putlog holes to hold the timber coffin supports had been built into each of the side walls, they had been put in at different levels! Four Victorian gully bricks standing on end had to be used as makeshift supports for the coffin. Finally, the overall construction was so poor that when the heavy ledger-stone was laid down to form the roof two vertical cracks appeared in one of the walls.

We do not know who these 19th-century cowboy builders were. Perhaps it was the grave-diggers themselves, engaging in a profitable little sideline. What is certain is that the 19th-century funerary trade, in all its aspects, offered ample temptation

A 'jerry-built' brick-lined grave. Buttresses were added to stop the walls of the grave collapsing outwards but instead they had started to collapse inwards.

to exploit the vulnerable, and this temptation was by no means always resisted. It is worth noting that the first burial in the jerry-built grave described above was that of a juvenile – is this a case of exploitation of grieving parents, or was the whole thing done in a rush on account of an unexpected death? On the whole, however, as in all things you no doubt got largely what you paid for.

If you got the right builder, a brick-lined grave was probably a good investment. The graves could be used to house not just one burial but several, stacked one on top of another. At St. Martin's the maximum was four (two examples), although two was most common, accounting for nearly half of the graves (ten examples), with single burials being the next most frequent (six examples). At least one of the brick-lined graves had been deliberately cleared out.

Although very variable, the preservation in the brick-lined graves was overall better than in the earth-cut graves. This meant that that there was quite often reasonable preservation of the coffin and coffin furniture, together with occasional preservation of funerary attire such as silk ribbons. One burial, in a 'fish-tail'-shaped coffin, included a tortoise shell hair slide. While Christian teaching does not encourage the deposition of personal items with the deceased, this injunction could be relaxed, particularly in the case of children. One grave with three burials, that of a sixty-five-year-old man, an 18-month old infant and a juvenile of about 11 or 12, included a complete necklace comprising some 300 pink glass beads attached to a copper-alloy pendant inlaid with a cut-glass rose. This looks very much like the treasured possession of a small girl.

We know the precise age of the man, John Sansom, and his infant granddaughter, Helen Mary Walker, because the coffin plates for these two individuals survived in a legible state. Helen had died in 1862 and John in 1873. Unfortunately we do not know the name of the juvenile associated with the glass beads, whose age is estimated from the skeletal evidence. Having details such as the name, age and date of death means that we can often trace something of the life story of individuals using such sources as burial records, trade directories, obituaries and wills. This provides some fascinating insights into life in 19th-century Birmingham and we will have another look at John Sansom, a retail brewer, in Chapter 11.

Two other brick-lined graves contained coffin plates that were legible or partially legible. One of these brick-lined graves was an unusual variant of the type. Rather than being rectangular it was 'shouldered' or coffin-like in shape, and had been built in two stages separated by some interval of time. The lower build formed a chamber to receive a single burial, floored by the natural sandstone and sealed by a narrow barrelled roof, which had settled to a virtually flat level. This roof formed the floor of the upper chamber, again designed to receive a single burial but in this case roofed by three flat slabs. The quality of the brickwork of the upper chamber was noticeably inferior to that of the lower chamber.

The burial in the upper chamber was very poorly preserved, with only fragments of coffin wood, coffin grips and a coffin plate. In the lower chamber, however, the coffin survived relatively well, together with fragments of its fabric covering and an oval coffin plate. The coffin plate was badly corroded so that only elements of the script could be read – *Sarah Parker ... Died November ....* Because we do not have the date of death we don't know who this Sarah Parker was. The National Burial Index lists three Sarah Parkers as having been buried in St. Martin's during November, in 1777, 1790 and 1825. The last date is the most likely to refer to the Sarah Parker in question but we cannot be certain.

The third brick-lined grave containing a 'named individual' was well-built and of standard design. It contained two adult burials in wooden coffins, one on top of the other. The lower coffin was in a very poor state of preservation but the upper one, although collapsed, bore a coffin plate declaring its occupant to be '*Captain Adjutant Benjamin Robinson Died June 5th 1834 Aged 60 Years*'. We will explore a little of the life of this interesting military gentleman in Chapter 11.

The brick-lined graves not only set their occupants apart from the herd, they also provided a good measure of security from disturbance. Although the brick-lined graves were found in various states of preservation and collapse (usually reflecting the quality of their construction), it was clear that they afforded effective protection against disturbance by later burials. The grave diggers and the builders of later vaults worked round them.

Fear of disturbance by other burials was perhaps not the only reason for wanting the security of a brick-lined grave. In the early 19th century the fear of body snatchers, the so-called 'resurrection men', was real. Body snatching, as is well known, took place in order to supply fresh corpses to medical schools for anatomical study; its most notorious practitioners were Edinburgh's 'Burke and Hare'. It is not known how real this threat would have been in Birmingham, but we know from contemporary accounts that it was believed to have occurred at the Cannon Street Baptist Chapel. The practice ceased with the Anatomy Act of 1832, which legalised the dissection of paupers' corpses for medical research. A less well-known reason for grave robbing was to obtain teeth, which were supplied to dentists for the manufacture of dentures. Such teeth were often called 'Waterloo teeth' due to the large numbers which were apparently extracted from corpses on the field of Waterloo in 1815.

Keeping it in the family: vaults

The third type of burial found in St. Martin's churchyard was burial in a brick-built vault. Eleven burial vaults were uncovered during the excavations, although one was not fully excavated; no more excavation was carried out than was absolutely necessary to facilitate the landscaping works. For our purposes we have defined the difference between a brick-lined grave and a vault as being that the latter has provision for at least two burials to be placed side by side in the structure with the possibility of stacking more on top. However, it may be a mistake to interpret this distinction too rigidly; they are both variations on a theme. All the available evidence suggests that the vaults were family tombs, with the possible exception of one, which was much larger than the others and of wholly different design.

While the size and design of the vaults varied it is possible to describe the construction of a typical example, which bears obvious resemblance to the construction of a barrel-roofed brick-built grave. A rectangular pit was dug down through the soil to the surface of the natural sandstone and lined with brick walls that could be one, two or on occasion three skins thick. The brick roof was of barrelled construction. Interior effects and features included whitewashing the walls and incorporating putlogs in the brickwork to take coffin supports and provide ventilation. Low internal divisions of bricks, stone slabs or, in one case, wood generally divided one burial from another.

The size of the vaults varied between about 2.6m to 4.2m length and about 2.0m to 2.8m in width; they were up to 3.5m deep. The same variation in the quality of construction was found in the vaults as in the brick-lined graves and the use of

A typical vault built with a double skin of brickwork. It originally had a barrel roof but this has been removed following collapse. The entrance is sealed with a slab of slate.

recycled bricks was also noted. Most of the vaults displayed various little idiosyncrasies of construction, including a couple of examples with 'composite' roofs of barrel vaulting and slabs. When uncovered by the archaeologists the vaults themselves and the burials within them were in various states of preservation; in two cases the roof had collapsed.

One vault, the largest and most elaborate found at St. Martin's, was of very different design to the others and may be described as a 'chambered vault'. It comprised four vaulted burial chambers served by an access corridor that ran the length of the structure. Entry was obtained by means of a set of steps at one end of the corridor. The tomb was built of multiple skins of clamped red bricks laid in header, stretcher and other decorative courses, bonded with a lime mortar. Analysis of the brickwork suggests a mid 19th-century date. Unlike the other vaults, the walls had not been whitewashed. Many of the bricks used were recycled; those that were heavily blackened had presumably been taken from chimney breasts. Two circular openings in the roof appear to have served as air vents. The interior of the vault displayed several interesting features, including brick coffin supports, iron fixings and mortar candle holders. These last evoke a scene of coffins being manoeuvred into position by flickering candle light.

The construction of the chambered vault at St. Martin's must have involved a great deal of planning and considerable expense. It seems to date to the very height of what we might call the 'Victorian burial crisis'. Unfortunately we don't know who commissioned the project – did four families get together on this, one for each chamber, or was it the work of a speculative developer who sold off the 'units'? The burials found in the tomb don't help us much.

Descending into the tomb by the steps and along the access corridor, the four burial chambers are on one's right. (The archaeologists were not the first people to enter this vault since the burials had been made – it had evidently been visited before as all the chamber entrances had been breached just enough to get a glimpse of the burials inside.) The first chamber contained nine burials, all in a poor state of preservation. Only one of the coffins preserved a coffin plate that was partially legible. It was of one James Cookley, who died at the age of 83 on the 20th February 18?? – the last part of the date is missing. Moving onto the next chamber, there were four adult burials, all in a fairly poor state of preservation, although it could be seen that the coffins were of lead shells with cloth covering and a wood lining. The next chamber contained five adult burials in a comparatively good state of preservation. However, on only one coffin was there a coffin plate sufficiently intact to be partially legible. It was of one Daniel Rowlin who died on 'March 30th …' – the year has gone.

Also in the third chamber was a burial that included a most interesting find. The deceased had worn a gold 'mourning ring' bearing the words 'Mr THOS. MARTIN DIED 13 SEP 1808 AGED 53'. This ring was not worn by Thomas

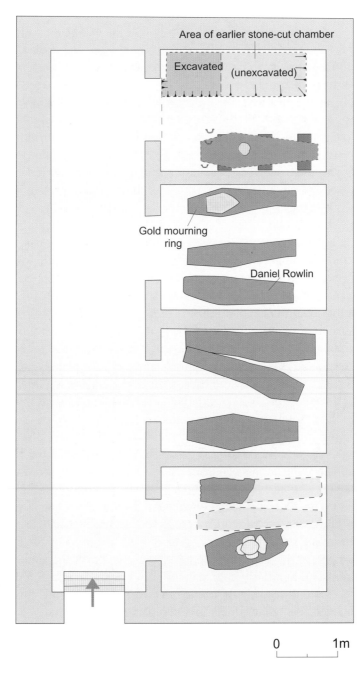

Area of earlier stone-cut chamber

Excavated   (unexcavated)

Gold mourning
ring

Daniel Rowlin

0   1m

A schematic plan of the large chambered vault. Only the bottom layer of burials is shown.

Martin himself but by somebody who held him dear – a relative, friend or admirer. Mourning rings were popular in the 18th and 19th centuries when they were commissioned in batches and given out at funerals as a form of commemoration and remembrance; Samuel Pepys (d.1703) made provision in his will for 129 mourning rings to be given away at his funeral. During the reign of Victoria, and particularly after the death of Albert, mourning rings became very popular and elaborate but the Thomas Martin ring is of a relatively simple design. The hallmark shows it was of London manufacture. At first the archaeologists assumed that the body wearing the ring was probably Thomas Martin's wife (make what you will of this assumption!) but it turned out to be wrong. When Dr Megan Brickley and Dr Helena Berry examined the skeleton in detail they concluded that it was of a male who had died somewhere between the ages of 35 and 55. As to Thomas Martin himself, research failed to find any record of him.

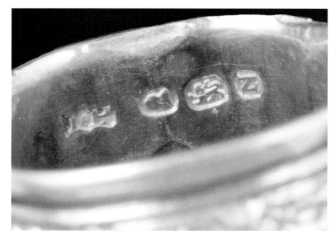

The gold mourning ring dedicated to Mr THOS. MARTIN DIED 13 SEP 1808 AGED 53. The hallmark shows that the ring is of London manufacture.

The fourth and final chamber contained only a single adult burial in a poor state of preservation. However, cut into the natural sandstone floor of the chamber were the infilled remains of an earlier chamber, which was presumably a stone-cut tomb. Upon excavation no bones were found, but this stone-cut chamber is a reminder that the graves excavated at St. Martin's only 'scratch the surface' of the range of burials that had once taken place in the churchyard.

The chambered vault aside, the number of burials in the nine other vaults excavated at St. Martin's was variable, from a minimum of three to a maximum of fourteen. We will describe the vault of the Warden and Browett families (linked by marriage) in some detail to show how the system of stacking of coffins in the vaults worked, and also to provide an indication of the range of evidence which survived in a well-preserved vault.

The Warden/Browett vault was the only vault that could be associated with a gravestone on the surface prior to excavation. The gravestone listed three names: Joseph Warden, Sophie Warden and Edwin Warden. The vault was very well built, with a triple skin of clamped red bricks bonded with a hard cemented mortar. The exterior dimensions of the vault were 2.8m by 2.9m. There were 14 burials in the vault, 13 adults and one juvenile. The coffins were stacked in four levels, with three or four coffins side by side on each level. The levels were divided by sandstone slabs laid on timber and iron floor supports. Vertical sandstone slabs, which also played

The burial vault of the Warden and Browett families.

a role in supporting the floors, subdivided each of the lower two levels into two compartments, a smaller compartment containing a single coffin and a larger compartment containing two coffins. In the upper two levels there were four coffins each and subdivisions were not clearly apparent.

Although the coffins had partially collapsed, the preservation in the vault was sufficiently good that the names and dates on five coffin plates could be read or partially read:

Name	Age	Date of death
Ann Maria Browett	81	8th April 1894
A(lfred) Browett		184?
Ann Maria Warden	52	17th February 184?
George Warden	33	26th November 1863
Sarah Emma Warden	47	14th December 1866

Using this information as a starting point it has been possible to reconstruct something of the intimate history of these two families from documentary sources. The results of this research are described in Chapter 11.

The preservation in the Warden/Browett vault was also such that the construction of the coffins and the design of the coffin fittings could be studied in detail, and a wide range of textiles survived, including wool coffin linings, funerary garments trimmed with silk and satin, and silk hair ribbons. A rare example of a face cloth trimmed with silk ribbon was also present. These are all material evidence of the 19th-century 'funerary trade' in Birmingham, which we shall look at in the next chapter.

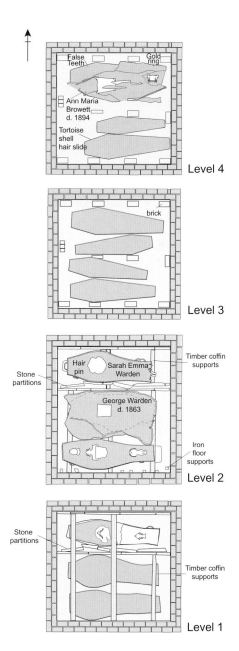

A schematic plan showing the four layers of burials in the Warden/Browett family vault.

The wedding ring of Ann Maria Browett was a plain gold band. The anchor hallmark shows it to be of Birmingham manufacture.

Other finds from the vault included, in addition to shroud pins and hooks, a number of hair accessories, including a hair pin, combs and grips, and a tortoise shell hair slide. Two finds associated with the body of Ann Maria Browett, who died in 1894 at the age of 81, deserve special mention. The first is a simple gold wedding ring. The hallmark shows this to have been of Birmingham manufacture and to date to 1835-6, when Ann Maria would have been about 22. This ties in perfectly with the documentary evidence, because we know that Ann Maria Warden married Alfred Browett on 26th July 1836. Not surprisingly the ring showed the effects of 60 years of wear. (This ring, as with all the other personal effects recovered during the excavations, has been reburied with its owner.)

Also found with the body of Ann Maria Browett was a complete pair of dentures. The dentures were made of Vulcanite, a derivative of rubber, and the false teeth themselves of porcelain (these were not the 'Waterloo teeth' mentioned above). Platinum pins held the teeth in place. The dentures were held in with a gold coil spring which linked the upper and lower sets. These early dentures, although they must have been very expensive, do not look at all comfortable and must have caused all sorts of problems with oral hygiene.

Four other vaults produced 'named burials' which have allowed family histories to be researched and reconstructed. These were the family vaults of the Jenkins family (recorded dates of death from 1827 to 1882), the Home family (1828 to 1833), the Ainsworth family (1827 to 1837) and the Haines family (1851 to 1904). The histories of these families provide a cross-section of middle class life in 19th-century Birmingham, which we will explore in Chapter 11. First, however, in the next chapter we will examine what light the excavation of St. Martin's churchyard can shed on funerary practices and the funerary trade in the town. With so many people dying, the trade was big business.

A pair of false teeth found in the coffin of Ann Maria Browett. The dentures are made of Vulcanite and the false teeth of porcelain.

Chapter 9

Dear Departed:
the Funerary Trade in Birmingham

Richard Cherrington with Simon Buteux

Birmingham in the 19th century was described as 'the city of a thousand trades'. The excavations at St. Martin's churchyard provide us with insights into a trade that few could do without. However, the funerary trade should not properly be thought of as just one trade – the death and burial of a dear one brought together in one chain of events a whole host of trades and professions. We can appreciate this by thinking through the process in its various manifestations and ramifications, although not all trades and professions will be relevant in every case: the doctor, the undertaker, the coffin maker (and behind him the timber merchant, the plumber [worker in lead] and the manufacturer and supplier of coffin fittings); the coffin furnisher and upholsterer (and behind them a host of textile workers and suppliers who made and supplied the coffin covers and linings, mattresses, pillows and sheets); the dress makers specialising in the supply of funerary garments and trimmings such as shrouds, bonnets, ribbons, bows and rosettes, and the makers of the pins to fix them; the florist; the sexton and the grave diggers; builders and stonemasons. This list, impressive though it is, is by no means exhaustive. It is restricted to those trades and professions which have left their mark, in one way or another, in the archaeological record at St. Martin's churchyard. Nevertheless, the list serves to show that the departed were not just dear in the sense of 'loved' but also dear in the sense of 'expensive'. And all this not to mention the costs of hearse and coaches; professional mourners, 'mutes', bearers and other attendants; sashes, bands and gloves; feasting and drinking – and lawyers.

In the 19th century the aristocracy and middle classes could spend a fortune on funerals. For the poor the cost of burying a member of the family could leave them destitute. It was a recognised social ill. The Bishop of Sodor wrote:

> '... a poor widow, left with hardly enough to put bread into the mouths of her children, was obliged to go to a great expense in order to bury her husband or a relative in (what is called) a decent way.'

We will examine the social and cultural aspects of the 19th-century funerary trade later in this chapter, but first we will take a brief look at each of the trades and professions mentioned and how they are exemplified in the archaeological record from St. Martin's.

Professions of death

The doctor

The medical profession potentially played two roles in the process of death and burial. First, although prohibitively expensive for most, doctors will have often been involved in attempting to treat or alleviate whatever illness or injury was the ultimate cause of death. We will learn something about the illness and injuries suffered by those buried at St. Martin's in the next chapter. A second role of the medical profession was on occasion to attempt to investigate the cause of death by autopsy. This was evident in several burials from St. Martin's that bore post-mortem surgical cuts around the top of the skull.

The coffin maker

For many funerals the coffin will have been the single most expensive item. The coffin is not a universal feature of burial. From the 16th to the late 17th century a reusable 'parish coffin' would have been employed for the burial of the poor. The shrouded body would have been transported to the grave side in the parish coffin before being removed and lowered into the grave. The absence of a coffin would have hastened the decay of the corpse and enabled the continued use of the graveyard for further burials.

In the 18th century burial in individual coffins became increasingly widespread. This marks a first step in the increasing elaboration of funerals, a first step in their increasing cost and the first flourishing of the funerary trade. For the poorest, burial in just a shroud probably continued into the 19th century; there were several examples amongst the earth-cut graves at St. Martin's of burials that seemed not to have been in a coffin, although evidence of a shroud was provided by the shroud pins. Unfortunately, it was very difficult to distinguish between those burials which had never been in a coffin and those where a coffin may have been present but had disintegrated completely. Certainly, very young infants were often buried just in a winding sheet.

The coffin maker, especially in the early years of the trade, was often not a specialist. Any cabinet maker or carpenter could turn their hand to the task. Early coffins for the poor would have been simple affairs with little or no elaboration. The coffins from the earth-cut graves at St. Martin's date mainly to the first half of the 19th century. Although often found in a very decayed state, they seem to have been predominantly single-case wooden coffins of 'single-break' type (i.e. the typical coffin shape). Where the type of wood used could be determined, which was only in 27 cases, it was predominantly elm, with occasional use of oak and pine. Elm is a cheaper wood than oak.

Coffins in the second level of the Warden/Browett family vault. All three coffins are of composite wood and lead construction. Partial disintegration of the central coffin has exposed the lead shell. The wood used was elm.

The coffins found in the brick-lined graves and the vaults were generally better preserved than those in the earth-cut graves although decay of the wood often made it difficult to determine their construction. A number of single-case coffins were identified in the brick-lined graves and vaults. This is surprising because, as we have seen, these graves were used for multiple burials spaced out over years and sometimes decades; coffins of a type which decayed rapidly, releasing liquids and gases, were therefore not advisable if the insertion of later burials was not to be an extremely unpleasant and distressing business (not to mention the health hazard). Double-case wooden coffins (i.e. coffins with two skins of wood) were also used, although this construction provided only limited extra protection from rotting. Best protection was provided by the use of a triple shell coffin with a lead shell sandwiched between two wooden shells. Elsewhere in the country, this type of construction is considered standard in vaults, and indeed was insisted upon by church authorities, so it is noteworthy that only about half of the coffins from the vaults at St. Martin's were of this construction. Also noteworthy is the fact that, as in the earth-cut graves, elm remained much the favoured wood for the construction of the coffins in the vaults, whereas one might have expected greater use of the more prestigious and expensive oak.

One coffin from St. Martin's churchyard deserves special mention. It is the coffin of Captain Adjutant Benjamin Robinson, who died on 5th June 1834, aged 60. Unlike all the other excavated coffins from St. Martin's where the shape could be determined, Captain Robertson's coffin was rectangular rather than the standard 'single-break' coffin shape. A rectangular coffin is the traditional mark of a military man. Apparently the tradition got started because when soldiers died abroad they were shipped home in rectangular boxes, which fitted best into the tightly-packed cargo holds.

The coffin fitting manufacturer

From the 18th century onwards a fairly standard range of metal fittings was attached to the coffins. These routinely comprised grips (handles) and grip plates on the sides of the coffin – usually six or eight in number – and the coffin plate on the lid. In addition, the assembly of the coffin and the attachment of coverings and linings required a range of nails, studs and screws.

Altogether 57 boxes-worth of such 'coffin furniture' was recovered from the excavations at St. Martin's. This is an important group because it represents a substantial sample of the products of the Birmingham 'toy trade' devoted to a single purpose and spread over the main period – the 18th and early 19th centuries – during which the toy trade flourished. At Park Street we saw the archaeological evidence for iron smithing and the manufacture of copper alloy articles in the earlier part of this period but virtually nothing was preserved of the products; it would not be too fanciful to imagine that some of them ended up buried in St. Martin's churchyard, only a stone's throw away.

We saw in Chapter 6 how the typical Birmingham manufactory of the late 18th century would produce a very wide range of goods – with Matthew Boulton's Soho Manufactory as the most famous example. Specialists in metal goods could include coffin furniture amongst their products. For example, in the Birmingham Directory of 1797 the firm of James Yates & Co. of Bradford Street is described as:

'Brass-Founders, and Platers of Coach and Coach Harness Furniture, Manufacturers of Coffin Furniture of all Sorts, also Looking Glasses, Picture Frames, Composition Ornaments, &c.'

The manufacture of coffin furniture was believed to have been introduced to Birmingham from London around 1760. Writing in 1781, one commentator observed:

'The manufacture of these articles, till very lately, was confined principally to the metropolis ... their introduction into this town, (but a very few years ago) has been attended with singular advantages. ... Artists of inventive minds and unwearied application, have called in the aid of dyes, presses and stamps. These have given an expedition to the execution of business, unknown, and unthought of before.'

Here we see the key characteristics of the Birmingham toy trade – endless invention and the effective use of simple machinery to produce a wide range of relatively low-price items. We may doubt that in 1781 the manufacture of coffin furniture had been introduced to Birmingham 'but a very few years ago'; the making of coffin fittings for local consumption at least is likely to have begun before this. What we are more likely witnessing is the first stage in the rise of Birmingham to become the premier national manufacturer of coffin furniture, supplanting London and other producers by the mid 19th century. As such it is just one facet of Birmingham's rise to industrial greatness. By 1829 the Birmingham firm of Yates, Hamper and Perry was also trading in 'Mercer's Street, Long Acre, London'.

The Birmingham coffin-fitting manufacturer produced a wide range of articles, in a variety of metals and finishes, to suit all tastes and pockets. The bulk of the large collection of fittings from St. Martin's came from the earth-cut graves and unfortunately were in a highly corroded and fragmentary state. All the grips were of iron but the vast majority were too corroded to assess even the shape, let alone the decoration. Both the grip plates and the coffin plates were very fragmentary and none of the coffin plates could be read.

In the brick-lined graves and vaults the state of preservation of the coffin fittings was very variable; some had disintegrated almost to nothing, others were in excellent condition. The grips were mostly of copper alloy, in a variety of different sizes and designs, some highly decorated. The grip plates were also mostly made of copper alloy, but iron, lead and tin/nickel were also used. The most popular decoration on the grip plates was the winged cherub and a floral motif, both very elaborate. The winged cherub motif was popular from about 1740 to 1850. A much simpler, geometric design was popular in the late Victorian period.

The coffin plates also came in a variety of styles, with the shield by far the most popular shape. The more expensive examples were made of Britannia metal or brass, which was sometimes electro-plated or gilded. A heraldic convention governed the shape of coffin plates, with a shield denoting a boy or young man, a lozenge a girl or unmarried woman and so forth. At St. Martin's, however, this convention (which was generally on the wane from the early 18th century) was not followed, and the shield design was used for men, women and children alike. The origins of the wealth and status of Birmingham's middle classes had nothing to do with the medieval traditions to which the world of heraldry belongs.

Two examples of the more elaborate coffin plates attached to the coffins at St. Martin's.

The coffin furnisher

The coffins were furnished with textiles of various kinds. In the 18th and early 19th centuries it was common to cover the coffin with a black baize-like cloth, held in place with rows of dome-headed brass tacks. The handles and coffin plates would be fitted on top. A white metal 'coffin lace' was sometimes added as a trim. At St. Martin's remains of these coffin covers survived in only eight cases, all from the vaults.

Lining of the coffin was a more general practice. Fragments of coffin lining were found associated with coffins in both the earth-cut graves and in the brick-lined graves and vaults. The linings were held in place with iron and copper-alloy tacks. Tufts of cattle hair or, less commonly, horse hair found in the coffins are probably the remains of the stuffing used to pad the lining. In coffins from two of the vaults fragments of silk satin ribbon, with pinked (trimmed to a zigzag edge) and punched decoration, were also found and probably represent a trimming used to finish the lining. A fragment of mattress cover was found in one coffin and the corner of a pillow from another, both in vaults.

Finally, although not strictly part of furnishing the coffin, a winding sheet would be placed in the coffin. The body was laid on it and then the sheet was wrapped around the body. Fragments of winding sheets were found associated with numerous burials in both the earth-cut graves and the brick-lined graves and vaults.

The dress maker

The body was dressed for burial in a garment which, although still called a shroud, would by the 18th century be better described as a gown. It was a full-length garment, worn by both sexes, and often decorated with ruffles down the front. Various fragments of a felted fabric (known to the Victorians as 'shrouding flannel') incorporating seams and hems, or with attached ribbons, found in the vaults at St. Martin's are likely to be from such shrouds.

Occasionally the face of the deceased was covered by an ornamented square face cloth. A fine example of one of these, with a design incorporating hearts, circles, flowers and leaves, was found in one of the vaults. There were the occasional remains of headdresses too. Mention should also be made of the finds of silk ribbons, bows, covered buttons and rosettes that accompanied some of the burials.

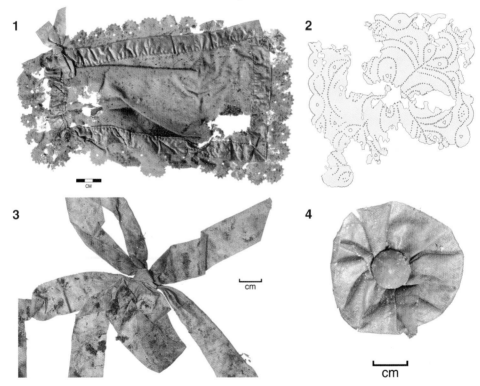

1. One of a pair of wool and silk items, possibly sleeve ornaments, from the Warden/Browett family vault. 2. A face cloth from one of the burials in the large chambered vault. Punched decoration with hearts and circles is used to form a floral pattern. 3. A festoon of decorative ribbon bows, from the Warden/Browett family vault. 4. A covered button rosette, from the Warden/Browett family vault.

The florist

Floral tributes were placed on the coffin, as they are today. Remarkably, remains of some of these tributes survived in four of the vaults. All that remained, however, were the tough leaves and twigs of the plants that probably formed the wreath – mainly evergreen trees or shrubs such as box, juniper and privet, although cherry was also found. If these wreaths were decorated with more delicate flowers, no trace of the latter remained. Box was most frequently found and has a long association with burial.

The grave digger, tomb builder and monumental mason

Little will be said of these as their work has been described in the previous chapter. However, it is worth emphasising that the construction of a vault must have been a major investment, and for poorer people even an earth-cut grave was a substantial outlay. The construction and engraving of a monument or gravestone was a further expense.

The undertaker

This profession has been left to last although for many an appointment with the undertaker will have been the first step in arranging the funeral of a relative. It has been left to last because in the whole business of burying the dead the role of the undertaker is a relatively recent innovation. There were myriad elements to a funeral in the 18th or 19th century, as we have seen, and we have only considered the archaeologically visible elements. In addition there were arrangements to be made for preparing and transporting the corpse, providing for mourners and generally orchestrating the funeral. Undertakers undertook to organise all this, but the profession could not really get going until two conditions were met – first, funerals had to become sufficiently complicated to require the services of an undertaker and, second, enough people had to require, and be able to afford, such services as to make the profession viable. Such conditions were not generally met until the 18th century, and the profession blossomed in the 19th century.

It appears that the undertaking business mainly grew out of the coffin making and upholstery trades, which themselves grew out of cabinet making and related trades. The enterprising individual undertook not just to do their own job – make coffins for example – but to do or organise the other aspects also. This meant that the various trades described above as if they were distinct activities could combine in various permutations.

The services of the undertaker particularly suited the needs of the entrepreneurial middle classes, who wished the ostentation of a lavish burial for their loved ones (or indeed for themselves) but lacked the time to organise it by themselves. This gave undertakers increasing control over the form and material requirements of a 'proper' funeral, inevitably driving up elaboration and expense. The less well off struggled to keep up. But the undertakers could provide the necessary financial services also, becoming increasingly involved in the formation and administration of 'burial clubs'. The idea of burial clubs was simple - through a weekly subscription one accumulated enough savings such that the club would both pay for one's funeral and leave money to help support one's dependents. Inevitably, however, the existence of such clubs meant that more money was spent on funerals than would otherwise have been the case, with little left over to support the family. The self interest of the undertakers was not hard to discern.

A backlash and reform movement followed. By the latter half of the 19th century voices were increasingly raised both against unnecessary pomp and cost of funerals and against the undertakers who encouraged it. The undertakers were seen as exploiting the poor and vulnerable in particular, by propagating the sentiment that a lavish funeral was the only way to show proper respect for a dead relative. One reformer wrote that it was 'a great pity that these widow-robbers cannot be discovered and punished for their nefarious traffic'.

The Birmingham Funeral and Mourning Reform Association was established in 1876 and sought to 'abolish unnecessary show and useless expenditure on the occasion of funerals, in the hope that by common consent a more simple and less gloomy ceremonial may be substituted'. It was appreciated that the burden fell hardest on the poor, and the middle-class members of the association were enjoined to lead by example and show 'that simplicity is not shabbiness, and that economy (for the sake of the living) is no dishonour to the dead'. The association offered its members a model wording to be included in their will:

'I direct my Executors to conduct my funeral in a simple and unostentatious manner, and that no plumes, velvet cloths, or trappings be used for the carriages or horses. And I request that those who attend the funeral wear no scarf, cloak, or long hatband, and that if any mourning apparel be worn after my decease, it be of the simplest kind.'

It is perhaps possible to witness the influence of the funeral reform movement in the archaeological record from St. Martin's churchyard. Where burials can be dated, a less elaborate style of coffin furniture seems to be associated with the later, post-1850 burials, the elaborate winged cherub and floral motifs being replaced by much simpler geometric designs.

Burial archaeology and society

The period from (say) 1760 to 1840 is that of the Industrial Revolution. It is no coincidence that this is also the period covered by the majority of burials excavated in St. Martin's churchyard. We have already seen from the excavations at Edgbaston Street and Park Street that the end of the 18th century is characterised by a transformation in the archaeological record, preceded by a lesser transformation in the earlier 18th century, physically marked by accumulations and deposits of 'dark earth' representing episodes of temporary abandonment, demolition and radical changes of land use. In the 18th century the face of Birmingham is changing and a thread of continuity from the past is broken, surviving only tenuously in a continuity of property boundaries.

In the archaeology of St. Martin's churchyard we witness a parallel transformation in the 'archaeology of the dead' as we see in the 'archaeology of the living' at the other Bull Ring sites. As burial had been carried out in St. Martin's since the medieval period, it is remarkable that the 18th- and, in particular, early 19th-century burials obliterated all but the merest hint of earlier burials (such hints are provided by, for example, the charnel pit into which was partially dug the earliest dated burial, of the 1720s). This obliteration is not just the effect of the normal process of reusing a churchyard, whereby earlier burials are progressively disturbed and destroyed by later ones – it is much more thoroughgoing than that. There were boxes and boxes of finds – mostly coffin furniture – from the 19th-century burials but not one find that could be confidently attributed to a grave preceding the 18th century. Of course in a sense this sharp distinction reflects little more than a change in burial practices – the 19th century burials were much more 'material' than those of earlier periods – combined with a hugely increased number of burials, but this is a fact of considerable significance in itself. It reflects a 'consumer revolution' that had affected all aspects of life and even death. Furthermore, in terms of visibility and monumentality if not in numbers, the 19th-century burials at St. Martin's are dominated by those of the middle-classes. Symbolically the brick-lined graves and, especially, the vaults do two things – they separate their occupants from the masses and they emphasise the importance of the family. On the surface, the now disappeared funerary monuments would have made these distinctions visible. The 19th-century saw the rise of the middle classes as the major force in society and it also saw the development of the ideal of middle-class family life: the archaeology of death at St. Martin's churchyard holds up a mirror to life.

Chapter 10

A Mirror to Life:
Analysis of the Human Remains

Megan Brickley

One of the ways in which the lives of the individuals buried in St. Martin's churchyard can be investigated is through the analysis of their skeletal remains. Each skeleton tells it own story and the information accumulated from the analysis of all the individuals taken together provides a unique insight into the lives of a cross-section of Birmingham's population in the 18th and 19th centuries.

The people excavated from St. Martin's are the largest group of individuals from this period to be excavated and analysed outside London. They are particularly important as they were living during the period of rapid social and economic change and development that we have learnt about in earlier chapters.

At the time of writing, analysis of the individuals and data gathered is still on going, but it is possible at this stage to provide some information on the first findings to emerge from these investigations. In many ways this information is unparalleled – skeletal analysis investigates areas of peoples lives often not written about directly in historical texts and most importantly it provides information on all individuals. In the next chapter where information from the historical records is discussed the fact that such sources mainly provide information on adult men becomes clear. In contrast, the analysis of skeletal material allows aspects of the life and death of men, women and children to be investigated.

The analysis of the skeletal material is being undertaken at the laboratories of the Institute of Archaeology and Antiquity at the University of Birmingham. Through the analysis of a relatively complete skeleton, it is possible to determine if the person was an adult or child and approximate age at death. The limitations of the techniques available mean that quite broad age categories have to be used, especially for adults. However, the information on age at death gathered is an invaluable source of information on mortality during this time period, and of the differences between men and women from various social classes.

People often think that life in the past was short with few individuals making it past the age of 40. Such misconceptions probably come from the average age at death being circulated and misinterpreted. The average age at death was indeed very low in the past, but this was largely due to very high levels of infant mortality, which were responsible for lowering the average age quite significantly. The high levels of infant mortality are borne out by the evidence gathered from the skeletal analysis. Almost a third of those excavated had not made it to adulthood, and the majority of these individuals died as babies and small children. When the adults were analysed, the largest age category was the 'older adults' and the number of individuals reaching old age is backed up by some of the information recovered from the coffin plates, for example the earliest dated burial, mentioned in Chapter 8, was that of an individual aged 85 years old at death. Other older individuals mentioned in the previous chapters were James Cookley, aged 83 and Ann Maria Browett who lived to 81.

Life was of course very different from today during the 19th century and far fewer individuals made it to such an old age, as medical conditions requiring modern medicines, or an emergency trip to the casualty department, would have been far more likely to have been fatal in the past. Another area where many lives are saved today is during childbirth – the risks associated with birth for both

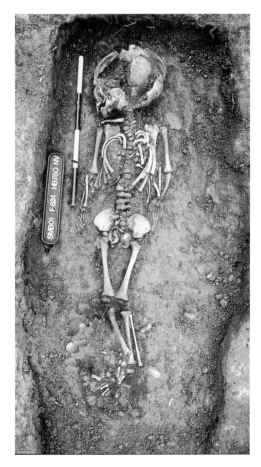

One of the many juvenile burials excavated from St. Martin's.

mothers and children without access to modern techniques is borne out by the discovery of a number of skeletons with fetal bones in the pelvic region. What needs emphasis – and what the data from the St. Martin's excavations demonstrates – is that we should not think of this period as one in which few adults made it to old age.

Other information that can be obtained from the analysis of skeletal material relates to the physical characteristics of the individuals and the types of disease and injuries from which they suffered. Not all diseases and injuries leave traces on the skeleton. For example the possibility of determining whether people died at the same time during an epidemic, something which probably happened frequently, would be difficult. The type of acute infectious diseases likely to kill people during an epidemic do not leave detectable evidence on the bones. With many such conditions, the individual dies far too quickly for any skeletal changes to occur. The main types of disease to leave a discernible mark are those which tend to be of long duration and not cause rapid death, for example conditions such as osteoarthritis, which are common today. The full analysis of the pathological conditions present will provide important information on the history and development of human disease. For example, one area being investigated is age-related bone loss and osteoporosis, a condition which today has serious consequences for many women. A clearer understanding of the history and pattern of development of this condition could contribute to a better understanding of the condition in today's population.

One of the most interesting aspects of the investigation of the human bone from St. Martins is the possibility of comparing the health of individuals from different social backgrounds – those from the vaults and brick-lined graves compared with those from the earth-cut graves. As noted in Chapter 7, there were health problems associated with the crowded urban living experienced by many of the individuals buried at St. Martin's, and the differences between the social classes are reflected in their skeletal remains.

The retreat of the middle classes from the filthy slum areas of the town centre to suburbs such as Edgbaston had a very marked effect on the health of the children of these families, and there is a stark contrast between health indicators recorded between the children buried in earth-cut graves and those from the vaults and brick-lined graves.

A number of indicators of health which can be investigated through the analysis of skeletal remains were studied, for example evidence of deficiency diseases such as scurvy (vitamin C deficiency) and rickets (vitamin D deficiency). The results were very interesting. The children buried in earth-cut graves, who would have come from working families living in the poor housing and overcrowded conditions of the town centre, had high levels of these conditions, especially rickets. In sharp contrast, those from the vaults showed very little evidence of these conditions. The prevalence of rickets, in particular, is very significant as it gives an insight into the environment and living conditions – even in Britain, a country not known for its abundant sunshine, almost all a person's daily requirement of vitamin D can be obtained through exposure of limited areas of the skin, such as the hands and face, to daylight.

It is known from contemporary accounts that the air pollution in the town, from industry and domestic chimneys, reached such appalling levels that at times it was sufficient to block out much of the sunlight. Another factor leading to the development of rickets would have been the type of housing that many poor people would have lived in. The town's poor would have occupied tightly-packed housing with small dirty windows and dark alleyways running between properties, and the conditions in many workshops would have been similar. A poor diet would also have exacerbated the problem, leading to the development of rickets in many children.

Vitamin D is vital for the formation of healthy bone as it is required for the proper mineralisation of bone. Without adequate levels of this vitamin bones do not form properly and softening of the bone leads to bowing and distortions. The changes associated with rickets are particularly marked in the bones of children as their rapid growth means problems related to bone formation are very soon apparent. However, it is not only in the young that deformity can be observed, marked deformity may persist in the bones of adults even after they have recovered from the condition.

Children from the vaults and earth-cut graves had different patterns of a range of other conditions, such as periosteal new bone formation (changes linked to infection), indicating that overall the children from earth-cut graves had higher level of chronic conditions associated with inadequate diet and poor levels of health and were less able to survive more acute infections.

When the adult skeletons from both the vaults and the earth-cut graves were examined the pattern of pathological changes found was very different to that in the children. Levels of many conditions which would give an indication of the past health of these individuals were the same in both groups of adults. For example, there was no difference in the levels of bone deformities due to rickets in childhood.

This pattern of differences in health between adults and children is very interesting. Like Joseph Warden, whose life is discussed in Chapter 11, many of the older adult individuals buried in the vaults would have been part of the new entrepreneurial middle class. Their origins may have been similar to that of many

The femur (thigh bone) of a child with evidence for rickets and the femur of an adult still showing residual changes associated with the condition.

of the adults buried in the earth-cut graves and this is reflected in some of the conditions they suffered from (although it should be noted that many, including Joseph Warden, had immigrated into Birmingham from surrounding Midlands towns and villages). This evidence from the study of pathology in bones backs up historical evidence for considerable levels of social mobility. However, the move of families, such as the Wardens, to Edgbaston away from the crowded, dirty and squalid conditions of the town centre did have a positive effect on the health of the children of these families.

Although some evidence for differences in the general health of individuals from different social groups can be determined, the comparative wealth of those in the vaults did not spare these individuals from all of the grim realities of life in a 19th-century town. For example William Haines, a solicitor, had suffered from osteoarthritis of his right foot and hip. The condition may have affected more joints, but it was only in these areas that it had advanced to a stage where evidence was

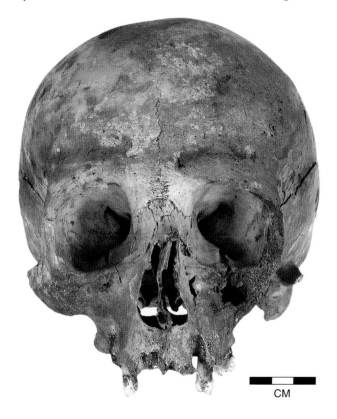

One of the adult male skulls from the vaults with a broken nose. The way the nose is broken suggests the blow was delivered by a right-handed assailant.

apparent on the bones. There was also evidence of an area of infection on his lower left leg. In addition, he had fractured his right wrist and had a broken nose! Fracture of the nasal bones can occur as a result of an accident, but more usually occurs as a result of violence. The fact that the nasal bones were displaced to the left may indicate that William was hit by a right-handed assailant. The fracture was well healed and so had not occurred in the recent past, but it is interesting to speculate about the types of social tensions that could have led this 'gentleman solicitor' and other gentlemen buried in the vaults to have sustained such an injury.

Although healed, the fracture of William Haines' wrist had not been well set and there was considerable displacement of the bones. Fractures are a relatively common finding in archaeological bone. For example, as well as suffering from broken ribs, Alfred Browett had fractured both his wrists. In the next stage of the project full analysis of the types of fractures and levels of healing will be investigated to shed light on the sorts of activities carried out by the various groups and on possible access to medical assistance. The successful treatment, or otherwise, of fractures is one area in which the efforts of the medical profession might be apparent in the skeleton.

At the time of writing, the full analysis of the human bone recovered from the vaults and earth-cut graves of St. Martin's is still at an early stage, but the information so far discovered is providing some fascinating insights into the lives and deaths of these past inhabitants of the town. Work still to be undertaken includes investigation of dental health, which provides an insight into diet and dental hygiene, fractures, and many of the infectious conditions such as tuberculosis and syphilis (through biochemical and physical examination), and biochemical analyses to investigate diet (stable isotope analysis). The full range of information produced by the investigations will be presented in the final monograph, which will provide a detailed analysis of demography, health and diet of a cross-section of Birmingham's population at a crucial period in the history of the town and, indeed, nation.

Chapter 11

Birmingham Lives

Jo Adams with Simon Buteux

A quarter of the burials in the excavated brick-lined graves and vaults at St. Martin's were found associated with coffin plates providing sufficient identifying information to enable research into their lives to be possible. The sources used for this research were varied, but included church burial registers, trade directories, census returns, obituaries and wills. In each case it was possible to produce some sort of portrait of their life, sometimes just a rough outline sketch but at other times a picture with rather more detail and colour. This put flesh on the bones and brought us closest to the lives of some of those buried in the churchyard. The fact of being able to examine the physical remains of these individuals and members of their families, together with having the details of the manner of their burial and some idea of their lives often gave a peculiar sense of intimacy. Below we provide some examples of these lives, organised according to the occupation of each individual.

The iron merchant

In Chapter 8 we described in some detail the vault of the Warden and Browett families, who were linked by marriage. The vault contained 14 burials, five of which could be identified from the coffin plates – Ann Maria Browett, Alfred Browett, Ann Maria Warden, George Warden and Sarah Emma Warden. In addition, the gravestone associated with the vault listed three further names – Joseph Warden, Sophie Warden and Edwin Warden.

The central figure in these two families was Joseph Warden (1787–1856). There was no surviving coffin plate with his name on it in the vault, but his body has been tentatively identified using the skeletal evidence in combination with documentary sources. As an iron merchant he is a representative of one of the most typical of Birmingham trades.

Joseph Warden came from Bulkington, to the northeast of Coventry, and moved to Birmingham as a young man. He was thus one of numerous immigrants from the area around Birmingham who came to the town to make their fortune, and were in large measure responsible for the rapid growth of the population of Birmingham in the early 19th century. Joseph married Ann Maria Marston on April 28th 1812 and on the birth of their first daughter, Ann Maria, in 1813 was described as an ironmonger.

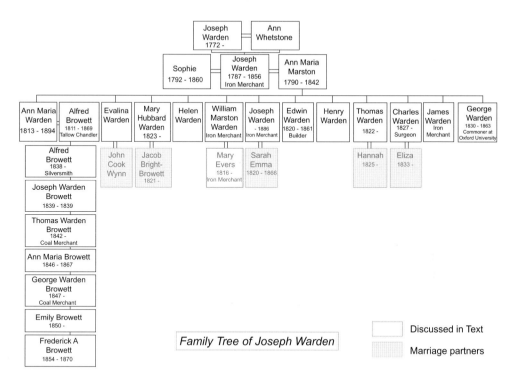

Family Tree of Joseph Warden

Discussed in Text

Marriage partners

A simplified family tree of the Warden and Browett families. The central figure in the tree is Joseph Warden, who with his first wife Ann Maria had twelve children. The children of his eldest daughter, also called Ann Maria, are also shown.

In the early 19th century an ironmonger's shop was a vital part of the community supplying a huge variety of goods from screws and latches to lighting and heating fixtures, cooking appliances, cycles and sports goods. They often had workshops on the same premises as the shop, where some manufacturing and repair of goods would take place. Consequently, tinware, copper and japanned ware, along with many small household items, like saucepans and kettles, may have been produced. In some shops the manufacturing aspect of the business became more important. It would seem that Joseph progressed from being a shopkeeper because in 1825 he is described in the trade directories as an *'ironmaster'* trading as Warden & Marston, at 14 Smallbrook Street. This would seem to be a partnership between Joseph and his wife's family, which was initially described as an *'iron merchants'*, but changed shortly afterwards to *'iron and steel merchants'*. In 1829 he is listed as the sole trader and from 1835 the description included tin plating and the business premises had moved to 5 & 6 Edgbaston Street. This illustrates diversification and expansion as Joseph adapts to the changing market that occurred as industrialisation in the town increased. In 1842, the business name changed to 'Joseph Warden & Son' to include William and, in 1846, it was 'Joseph Warden & Sons' as Thomas joined the family firm. The family firm was further strengthened in 1854 as sons Joseph and Thomas formed a partnership with Benjamin Williams. This lasted for 21 years at Oak Farm Ironworks, illustrating something of the enduring quality of a firm that started as an ironmonger's shop at the beginning of the century.

While Joseph's business was prospering, he and his wife brought up twelve children. To accommodate this growing family, and reflecting his increasing wealth, Joseph and his wife moved to Wellington Road, Edgbaston. The fact that all twelve children survived to be adults was remarkable for this period. The move to Edgbaston, away from the dirt and squalor and annoyances of the old part of town, was characteristic of men like Joseph who had started living 'over the shop' but had made their fortune in trade. A poem by H H Horton captured the trend:

JOSEPH WARDEN & SONS,
IRON, STEEL, AND TIN PLATE MERCHANTS,
EDGBASTON STREET, BIRMINGHAM,
MANUFACTURERS OF
PATENT RAILWAY SPIKES AND BOILER RIVETS;
ANVILS, VICES HAMMERS, TUE IRONS, BELLOWS,
SCREW AND WIND-UP JACKS;
SPADES, SHOVELS, TYRE, SPRINGS,
IRON ARMS, AXLE-TREES, HURDLES,
HAMES, CHAINS, FILES, NAILS, &c., &c.

This advertisement for 'Joseph Warden & Sons' shows the wide range of products manufactured by the firm.

By his later years Joseph Warden had become a wealthy man and like many other successful merchants bought a fine house in Edgbaston. This is Joseph's house on Wellington Road today.

'See Edgbaston, the bed of prosperous trade,
Where they recline who have their fortunes made.'

After Ann Maria died in 1842, aged 52, Joseph married Sophie who lived with him at his house on Wellington Road, where she died in 1860, aged 68.

Joseph himself died aged 69 on 25th January 1856 at the house on Wellington Road. He had during his lifetime risen from running a small ironmonger's shop quite close to St. Martin's Church in Smallbrook Street, to owning a large iron workshop in Edgbaston Street, nail shops in Gloucester Street and, as his will reveals, a factory on Gas Street, a foundry and some shops that had also been used as a wharf. His is the archetypical success story of the entrepreneurial Birmingham middle class.

The iron merchant's daughter

There is not the space here to follow in detail the careers of all Joseph Warden's twelve children (these may be pursued in the monograph on the St. Martin's churchyard excavations). Four of the sons followed their father's trade of iron merchant, either in the family firm or setting up for themselves. Another became a builder. Showing the upward mobility of the family, Joseph's last child, George, went to study at Worcester College, Oxford University. He died there in 1863, aged 33, from opium poisoning. His death certificate states that he died from 'inadvertently taking an overdose of opium which he had used habitually for the last two years to relieve neuralgia pain'. The taking of opium was common practice at the time but we may question whether George used it solely for medicinal purposes. An earlier student at Worcester College, the essayist Thomas de Quincey, also took opium, both as a remedy for neuralgia and because 'here was the secret of happiness about which philosophers had disputed for so many ages'.

Of the lives of Joseph's four daughters, we shall describe just that of his eldest, Ann Maria. Ann Maria is one of the 'named burials' in the Warden/Browett vault. She lived to the age of 81, and it was in her coffin that were found her wedding ring and false teeth (see Chapter 8). Also found in her coffin were two fragments of black silk, probably ornament from a garment worn in life. One fragment bore a motif in a style that suggested that the garment was a little out of fashion when she died.

Ann Maria was born in February 1813 to Joseph and Ann Maria Warden, who then lived on Bristol Street. She was named after her mother suggesting that she was their first daughter and, 33 years later, was to follow the same tradition and call her own first daughter by the same name.

On 26th July 1836 she married Alfred Browett, the son of William Browett, who was a draper and had moved from Stoke, a small village in the Coventry area. Alfred worked with his father in a shop at 47 Smallbrook Street. This was described in a trade directory of 1833 as a *'grocer, tea dealer and chandler'*. Over the ensuing years this description varied. In 1842 it is listed as *'chymist and druggist'* in Jamaica Row and, in 1849, the business returned to Smallbrook Street, with the added description of *'cheesemonger and maltster'*. This shop, like the ironmongers that Ann Maria grew up in, was situated close to St. Martin's in an area of small crowded streets, full of a variety of shops. These shops included butchers, nail makers, umbrella makers and jewellers, all very close to the markets from where supplies would have been readily available. Many shops also had the facility for small-scale manufacturing. Joseph Warden may have had a small forge and foundry in his ironmongers; Alfred may have had facilities for processing cheese. Alfred was described primarily as a *'tallow chandler'* and would probably also have made candles and soap, both vital commodities in the Victorian household. He would, therefore, have been subject to the same taxes and excise restrictions as a soap boiler, who had to inform the excise officers twenty-four hours before making soap.

It is impossible to know whether Ann Maria helped Alfred in the shop. However, women were more actively engaged in the retail trade than any other, so it may have been a possibility at the beginning of their married life.

In 1849 William Browett's name disappears from the shop title. This suggests that either he has died or has retired from the business, leaving his son in charge. The family may have lived over the shop during the first part of their married life, as the lock-up shop was still unusual in 1850. However, in the 1851 Census they are listed as living on Bristol Road.

By 1851 Ann Maria and Alfred had five children. Alfred, aged 13, and Thomas, aged 9, are described as *'scholars'*, while George aged 4 is listed as a *'scholar at home'*. In contrast young Ann Maria, aged 5, has no such description, indicating that she does not seem to be receiving any tuition at all – a clear illustration of the attitude to girls' early education at the time. They also employed a nursemaid and cook, who were born in Westbury-on-Severn and Bromsgrove respectively. This again illustrates the migration which was occurring at the time, as people moved from rural areas into the town to find employment. The family's ability to employ two servants also gives some indication of their level of income.

Further proof of financial stability is indicated in the 1861 Trade Directory, where Alfred is still described as a *'tallow chandler'* at 47 Smallbrook Street, but now listed as living at 9 Yew Tree Road in the fashionable suburb of Edgbaston. The house was not one of the biggest in Edgbaston, but had a garden back and front and was close to neighbouring streets where the more affluent Birmingham families lived, in rather larger properties. The two eldest boys are now at Commercial College and the 15 year-old daughter (Ann Maria) and the 14 year-old son (George) are described as *'scholars'*. There are three other children, Emily, aged 11, Evalina, aged 9, and Frederick, aged 7. The family still had help in the house, with two domestic servants aged 16 and 19. By this time the couple had seven surviving children, Joseph having died in 1839 aged 3 months.

In 1867, Ann Maria's daughter, her namesake, died and, on 16th March 1869, her husband Alfred died at home after being ill for a month with Phthisis, a progressive wasting disease. Alfred was buried in the Warden family vault, thus uniting in death two families who must have been close in life. DNA analysis has confirmed that he died from tuberculosis. He had probably worked long hours in the shop all his life. Opening times varied but often they stayed open 12 to 16 hours per day and longer on Fridays and Saturdays. Hours were extended in the summer and those shops catering for the working classes, as Alfred's would have done, would also have been open longer. The shop may have been small and badly ventilated, all of which may have contributed to the cause of his death. This illustrates that despite a relatively high standard of living for the middle classes, the fear of fever, cholera and consumption was an ever-present threat in the growing industrial cities.

It would seem that none of Alfred's sons took over the shop since the eldest, also called Alfred, became a silversmith in Dean Street, and George and Thomas became *'coal and brick manufacturers'* in the town. The family still lived in Yew Tree Road in 1870 and on 20th September of the same year Frederick died. At some time in the next ten years the family moved and Ann Maria settled in a house in Greenfield Crescent, Edgbaston, where she and her daughter, Evalina, are listed in the 1881 Census as lodgers, with an income from a house in Leamington.

By 1894 Ann Maria has moved again, to 185 Bristol Road. This is near to where she lived as a child and she died there on 8th April, aged 81. Her death was attributed to chronic bronchitis, which she had suffered from for some years, and senile decay. At the time of her death she still had the leasehold of a property in Leamington, three of her sons were businessmen in the town, her daughters Emily and Evalina were married and two of her children had pre-deceased her. She was buried in a vault at St. Martin's along with other members of the Browett and Warden families that had been first united by her marriage to Alfred 58 years before, in 1836.

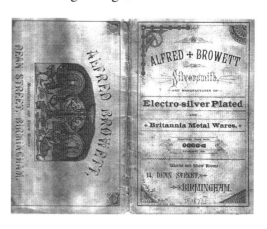

Ann Maria and Alfred Browett's first son, also called Alfred, became a silversmith. This is the trade catalogue for his business on Dean Street.

The house on the Bristol Road where Ann Maria Browett died on 8th April 1894.

18_44_	DEATHS in the Sub-District of _Eagleston_					in the Count_ies_ of _Birmingham & Worcester_			
	(Col. 1.)	(Col. 2.)	(Col. 3.)	(Col. 4.)	(Col. 5.)	(Col. 6.)	(Col. 7.)	(Col. 8.)	(Col. 9.)
No.	When and Where Died.	Name and Surname.	Sex.	Age.	Rank or Profession.	Cause of Death.	Signature, Description, and Residence of Informant.	When Registered.	Signature of Registrar.
241	Eighth April 1894 185 Alexandra Road Eagleston Birmingham	Ann Maria Browett	Female	81 years	Widow of Alfred Browett a retired Soap Manufacturer	Bronchitis (Chronic) some years Senile decay Certified by Charles Warden M.D.	Emily Wynne Daughter present at the Death Northfield July Q. Oxfield	Eleventh April 1894	Edward Baker Registrar

The death certificate of Ann Maria Browett, 1813-1894.

With the exception of Ann Maria Browett, all the Birmingham people described in any detail in this chapter are men. This reflects both Victorian attitudes and the nature of the records available, which conspire to keep women somewhat 'invisible'. However, the huge changes in society that were a consequence of increasing industrialisation dramatically affected women's lives. The role of the women depended largely upon their status. Not many women conformed to the archetypal Victorian ideal of women being 'gentle, submissive, passive, self sacrificing domestic creatures, an ideal largely inspired by Queen Victoria's example'. This may have been the case amongst some of the wealthier families, but other women were an integral part of the family unit, not only as a mother, but also as a wage earner or as unpaid support in the family business. (It is noteworthy that Mary, the widow of Ann Maria's brother William, was described in the 1851 Census as 'head of household and iron merchant', suggesting that she had taken over her husband's role.)

At first glance it would seem that Ann Maria Browett lived an unremarkable life. She was born in 1813, got married aged 23, had 8 children and lived, until her death in 1894 in Edgbaston, not having moved more than a few miles from where she was born. However, this lady, who lived for 81 years, witnessed unprecedented changes that occurred in Birmingham, in Britain and indeed in the lives of contemporary women.

The brewer

John Sansom was buried in a brick-lined grave along with the remains of Helen Mary Walker, his 18-month-old granddaughter. The other burial in the grave was of a juvenile of about 11 or 12, touchingly buried together with her necklace of pink beads (see Chapter 8); her identity is not known but it is possible that she was another of John Sansom's grandchildren. That he was a kind man who cared for his grandchildren is something that emerges from his will.

John Sansom was born in 1808 in Bilston, Staffordshire and married Eleonor from Perry Barr, Birmingham, on 26th July 1830 at St Philip's Church. He was a *Retail Brewer* in Sherbourne Road, Kings Norton in 1861. The number of these small retail outlets selling beer had increased dramatically in the town after the 1830 Beerhouse Act. This Act abolished beer duty and allowed any householder assessed on the poor rate to obtain an Excise licence for 2 guineas, to sell beer from his own house, either as an on or off sale. The householder did not have to make any application to the Justices but was subject to restricted opening hours. The reason behind the Act was an attempt to control the growing problem of spirit drinking. It was thought that these small establishments would draw people away from the alehouses and inns where spirits and beer were both sold. However, the Act had the reverse effect as more and more of these small drinking houses appeared and drunken behaviour increased. In subsequent years the government introduced further Acts of Parliament to control the problem, and by the time John moved from Birmingham to Leamington Spa in 1871 he would have had to adhere to much more stringent rules to become the *Licensed Victualler* at 95 Brunswick Street. This was the address of the Queen's Head that was run in 1874 by George L Sansome, another member of the family. It was in Leamington that John died on 3rd March 1873, aged 65.

His body was brought back from Leamington to St. Martin's Church to be buried, possibly because there was a family grave available. His will was written in 1870, three years before he died, and was extremely thorough. He had stocks and shares and various trusts with a total value under £1000. His beneficiaries were his wife and his daughter Ann, who married Samuel Walker and lived in Balsall Heath. The reference to his daughter displayed a caring character, reflecting perhaps the change in attitude towards women towards the end of the 19th century. He states that the bequest should be 'for her own and absolute use and benefit free from the debts power or control of her present or any future husband she may happen to have'. He also made provision for the education and maintenance for any grandchildren she may have and if Ann, his daughter, should die then it is the grandchildren, not the husband, that should have the money, when they reach 21.

The chemist

The lives of John and Frances Home cannot have been happy, and illustrate the reality of high child mortality in early 19th-century Birmingham.

John and Frances Home are two of the earliest 'named' burials from St. Martin's, dying in 1828 and 1833 respectively, at the ages of 50 and 53. They were buried in a well-built vault accessed by a bricked-in arched opening. The vault was subdivided internally by a 1m-high brick partition wall, braced to one of the walls of the vault by metal straps. On one side of the partition were the coffins of John and Frances Home. They were both buried side by side in composite lead and wood coffins. The elm wood outer shell of John's coffin still retained a covering of green fabric decorated with brass studs. The coffin plate, coffin grips and grip plates were still intact. The inner lead shell was of a fish-tail design and had an incised diamond pattern on the outside.

On the other side of the brick partition were very disturbed and fragmentary skeletal remains of two individuals, a juvenile and an infant; the coffin only survived as a spread of decomposed wood fragments. These are probably the remains of two of John and Frances' children, Sophia Frances, who, we learn from deaths listed in *Aris's Gazette* (the Birmingham newspaper of the time), was aged 12 when she died in January 1817, and Edward, who was only 8 months old when he died in March of the same year.

Because of the early date of their deaths (they both died before Queen Victoria's accession to the throne in 1837), fewer lines of documentary research were available on the lives of John and Frances Home than was the case with the later burials.

John Home was a *'chemist and apothecary'* or *'chemist and druggist'* from 1803 to 1825. For the majority of this time his place of business was 70 High Street, in the centre of the town, although briefly, in 1816, he moved to Union Street, before returning to High Street in 1818. It is possible that the Homes lived above the shop in the High Street but subsequently moved to the Bristol Road, where Frances lived alone after her husband died.

None of the Homes' children survived beyond 12 years of age. We have already mentioned Sophia Frances and little Edward, whose remains were probably buried in the vault with John and Frances. They also lost Mary, aged 1 year 7 months on 8th May 1816, Amelia, aged 9 on 23 February 1819 and Alexander, aged 5 months on 12 December 1823.

With some tragic irony, John Home's expertise as a chemist and druggist did not help save his children, nor was his own life a long one. Apothecaries, or chemists and druggists as they later came to be called, played an important role in the lives of ordinary people throughout the 19th century (and of course the trade goes back much further than that).

History from bottles

To illustrate the kind of medicines available we can turn to a rather surprising source of evidence – a number of bottles found amongst the rubbish filling a disused well at the archaeological site at Edgbaston Street. The bottles were dumped into the well about 1895, so are a good deal later than the period during which John Home was practicing, but they nevertheless provide an interesting perspective on the profession in Birmingham.

The medicine bottles, which formed part of a large collection of bottles formerly containing a variety of products ranging from mineral water to perfume, were studied by an archaeology student at the University of Birmingham, David Orton.

David pursued the history of the different firms whose names are embossed on the bottles. We can only give a flavour of what he found here.

Eight of the bottles found in the well could be attributed to seven chemists operating in the Birmingham area in the late 19th century. Here are some examples of the embossed texts, with notes:

DONE, CHEMIST BY EXAMINATION, SMALL HEATH
(James Done first appears in Kelly's Directory of Birmingham in 1875, based at 137 Coventry Road. Over thirty years he relocated his business to several new addresses on the Coventry Road and is last recorded in 1906. The term, 'chemist by examination', suggests that Done provided a service somewhere between that of a doctor and a normal dispensing chemist.)

TUBBS & WILKINS, 1 HOCKLEY HILL, BIRMINGHAM

SNAPE & SON, CHEMISTS, BIRMINGHAM
(Snape & Son is a company with a long history, still surviving at the end of the 20th century. The company began trading under the name of Edward Snape in the mid 19th century from premises on Great Hampton Street. Edward's son joined the company around 1869, and the company expanded to additional shops in Hamstead Road and Villa Road at the turn of the century.)

We do not know why so many medicine bottles should come to be thrown down a well around 1895, but the find does serve to underline the importance of self-medication in the 19th century, and many chemists, quacks and otherwise, did very well out of the business; the expensive vault and elaborate coffins of John and Frances Home bear testimony to this.

In 19th-century Birmingham, and particularly in the unsanitary, crowded working class areas, illness was an everyday fact of life. Going to the doctors was prohibitively expensive for many, so most turned to the chemists and druggists who would sell both their own medicines prepared in the shop and 'patent medicines' bought in from a supplier. The effectiveness of many of these concoctions is highly dubious (it wasn't until the 1941 Pharmacy and Medicines Act that manufacturers were required to disclose the active ingredients on the label). Amongst the medicine bottles from Edgbaston Street were several embossed with the name of a patent medicine, including a laxative, 'DINNEFORD'S SOLUTION OF MAGNESIA', advertised as 'the best mild aperient for delicate constitutions, being specially adapted for ladies, children and infants'.

Extreme claims were made for the effectiveness and range of application of some medicines. One example found in the well was a bottle which had contained

'Lamplough's Effervescing Pyretic Saline'. This concoction, which was sold as a powder and hence in a bottle with a wide neck, was not only claimed to provide instant relief for minor complaints such as headaches, sea or bilious sickness and constipation, as well as curing skin, liver and blood diseases, but also to treat serious diseases such as small pox, scarlet fever and typhus, all of which could be killers. Lamplough's Effervescing Pyretic Saline wouldn't have been on John Home's shelves but one rather doubts it would have helped his children anyway.

A late Victorian chemist's shop. The chemist provided an important service to poor people who could not afford a doctor.

An alternative was the herbalist approach. One bottle from the well was embossed with 'O. PHELPS BROWN, LONDON'. Whether or not Dr O. Phelps Brown's medicine was any more effective than Effervescing Pyretic Saline it must have gained some reputation because in 1875 he had published a book 'The Complete Herbalist: the People Their Own Physicians By the Use of Nature's Remedies' in Jersey City, New York.

The saddler

The Ainsworth family vault was located in the northwestern corner of the graveyard, close to the boundary wall. On excavation it initially appeared to contain only discarded coffin shells. However, further excavation revealed a number of poorly-preserved burials contained within some of these coffins. The coffins with legible coffin plates belonged to the middle layer of three. The layers had been separated by wooden beams that had rotted through, resulting in the collapsed state of the coffin material.

The named burials were of Hannah Ainsworth, who died on 1st January 1827, aged 68, and of Isaac Ainsworth, who died on 11th December 1837, aged 80. (It is noteworthy how many old people died in winter.)

Hannah and Isaac Ainsworth, a married couple, lived on St. Martin's Lane, one of the boundary roads around the church, where they had been married on 17th February 1782. Hannah had moved to the town from Inkberrow in Worcestershire where she was born in 1757 or 1759. Isaac was a saddler, a profession that was vital at this time to maintain the large number of horse drawn carts and carriages that formed part of daily life. By the 1840s Birmingham had the second largest concentration of saddlers and harness makers in the country, after London. It has been suggested that the number of carts, vans and wagons grew by 75%, to over 200,000, between 1811 and 1851, and the number of horses to two million nationwide, resulting in a huge potential market for saddlery and associated trades. There were many leatherworking establishments in the streets around St. Martin's (it is worth remembering here the archaeological evidence from Edgbaston Street), usually small domestic workshops employing two or three people to supply local demand. Some made just saddles, while other more specialist shops made whips, whip thongs and collars.

A saddler at work in the early 19th century.

It is possible, since they lived and worked at the same address, that Hannah and other family members contributed to the business, as women and children were often employed to cut, stitch and plait the leather.

Isaac and Hannah had a son, Isaac, who is almost certain to be buried in the vault. He died in 1821 at the age of 28 and is listed in the obituaries as living with his parents, but in the National Burial Index as living on nearby Moseley Street.

The soldier

We have already mentioned Captain Robinson, who died on 5th June 1834, aged 60; his coffin was of an unusual rectangular shape, which was the military tradition (see Chapter 9). He was the upper of two burials (the other unidentified) in a barrel-roofed brick-lined grave.

Captain Adjutant Benjamin Robinson was the son of Jonathan Robinson and Rebecca Harfield, a local couple who had married in 1769 in neighbouring Aston. He was christened in St. Martin's on 23 August 1773.

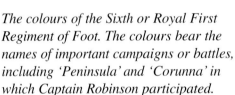

The colours of the Sixth or Royal First Regiment of Foot. The colours bear the names of important campaigns or battles, including 'Peninsula' and 'Corunna' in which Captain Robinson participated.

Soldiers of the Sixth or Royal First Regiment of Foot in 1838, shortly after the death of Captain Adjutant Benjamin Robinson.

He was a soldier who rose to the rank of Captain Adjutant in the 6th or Royal 1st Warwickshire Infantry regiment. Captain Robinson was involved in the Peninsula War, landing with his regiment in August 1808 where he became part of the famous retreat of Sir John Moore to Corunna. During this campaign 6,000 soldiers died and many others returned to England wasted and ill from the hardships they had had to endure. Then in 1809, when he was 35, he took part in the expedition to Walcheren, a small island off the Dutch coast. The object of this campaign was to capture Antwerp in order to prevent Napoleon from using it as a base for a future invasion of England. The expedition was not successful as the army became marooned on the island with 218 dying in action, 4000 dying of malaria, and another 11,000 ill when they were evacuated.

When Captain Robinson died he was living at Cheapside, very close to St. Martin's. His obituary in *Aris's Gazette* cited his military achievements and described him as 'filling the arduous position of Quarter Master to the 6th Regiment of Foot as part of the rear division' during Moore's retreat from Corunna.

His wife Elizabeth died before him in 1831 aged 55, and it is probable that she was in the coffin below him in the grave.

The lawyer

William Haines, his wife Jane and six of their children were buried in a vault originally surrounded by iron railings just outside the front entrance to St. Martin's Church. It is unclear whether this represents some sort of special privilege given his status in society or whether it was the only place left for a large vault in the crowded churchyard. Whatever the reason, he and his family had been associated with the church throughout their life. Both William and Jane were christened there in 1797 and 1804 respectively.

William, described as a 'Gentleman' and 'Solicitor of this town', was born on 13th January 1797, the son of William and Ann, while Jane's parents were James Busby and Lucy Lloyd, who also married in the church, on 29th December 1785. Jane's maternal grandparents were Sampson and Ann Lloyd who may have been related to the Lloyd family that, with the wealthy button manufacturer John Taylor, had opened Taylor and Lloyds Bank – later to become Lloyds Bank – in the town in 1765.

William and Jane married at St. Bartholomew's Church, a Chapel of Ease to St. Martin's Church, on 13th April 1826 and began their married life living at 48 Lower Hurst Street, near the centre of the town. By this time, William was already practising as a solicitor, having been first mentioned in The Law List in 1820.

He began practising at a time when the profession was undergoing considerable change as it sought to improve the reputation of the solicitor who, in earlier times had often been considered corrupt and of ill repute. The aspiration of the profession was to ensure that its practitioners were all 'gentlemen', and so knew how to conduct themselves. How the fact that William had broken his nose at some point, possibly in a fist fight, squares with this aspiration makes for entertaining speculation.

William was described as an *'Attorney & Solicitor'* and in 1821 worked in a partnership with John Arnold and W. Smith that was based in Lower Hurst Street, where William had his home. The firm evolved and moved to 2 Cannon Street in the centre of the town where it was known as 'Arnold and Haines' before moving to 86 New Street, when John Arnold junior joined his father.

The firm were also listed as Clerks to the Commissioners of the Birmingham Streets Act, which meant they acted on behalf of the Street Commissioners. As we saw in Chapter 6, this body was formed in 1769 and was charged, amongst other things, with sorting out Birmingham's chaotic markets and providing lighting to protect persons and property.

In his capacity of Clerk to the Commissioners, William Haines helped to implement some of their policies. In 1828 he was involved in the plans for the proposed new Market Hall and in 1844 he was involved in a court case concerning air pollution. On this occasion, a Mr Cadbury had complained to the Commissioners about smoke coming from a steam engine that belonged to Mr James Hughes in Broad Street. Mr Hughes had to appear at Warwick Assizes and was subsequently fined £500 plus £10 damages, and told to rectify the problem. He did not do this immediately and, after another report from the Inspectors, Mr Haines had to write again threatening him with more legal action. Mr Hughes eventually agreed to fit a new boiler and adapt the chimney so the problem was solved. This seemingly trivial court case (although £500 was a lot of money), as well as reminding us of some of the effects on health caused by industrial pollution in the town, noted in the previous chapter, illustrates another aspect of Birmingham industry, the employment of steam power for an increasing number of industrial processes. The partnership of Matthew Boulton and James Watt in the development of the steam engine in the last quarter of the 18th century is one of the most celebrated in the history of Birmingham and the history of technology. However, the nature and essentially small-scale workshop basis of many of Birmingham's trades meant that steam power does not seem to have played a major role in the industrial development of Birmingham until the 1830s and 40s. The 1844 court case involving William Haines thus symbolises a particular stage in Birmingham's development.

In 1849, William Haines was involved in preparing the evidence to put before the Inspectors for the enquiry into the sewerage, drainage, supply of water and the sanitary condition of the town.

As William's professional life progressed his private family circumstances changed too. He and his wife had more children and as he became more prosperous he, like many others, moved out of the centre of the town to more picturesque surroundings in Harborne. They lived at 57 Lodge Road, which became know as Harborne Lodge. He and his wife had nine children but sadly William, James and Alfred died before their second birthday. They had a staff of a housemaid, an underhouse-maid, a cook and a groom.

Towards the end of his life another indication of William's growing wealth was the acquisition of property in Small Heath and Kings Norton. He died in July 1851 aged 54, having suffered from general debility with *atrophia cordis* (heart problems) for nearly four years. As we learned in the previous chapter, he also suffered from osteoarthritis. According to his obituary in *Aris's Gazette* he was 'deeply lamented by his family and friends'.

The bedstead maker

Following the death of William Haines the family moved to 9 Vicarage Road in Harborne, where, ten years later, his widow Jane still lived with three of her children. Jane Lloyd Haines died on 21 January 1869. We don't have the space here to follow the careers of all William and Jane's children, but we will take a brief look at one of their sons, Campbell Lloyd Haines, because his career tracks the development of Birmingham industry – and because of his socks!

Campbell Lloyd Haines, unmarried at 25, was an architect and surveyor working at 70 New Street. In 1864 he diversified and invested in one of the growth industries of the day. Despite a period of economic depression in the town, the brass trade was still expanding, and in particular Birmingham was making a name for itself in the production of bedsteads. Campbell must have realised the potential and in 1864 became a partner in Hulse and Haines, a company that made brass and iron bedsteads in Icknield Street West. His death certificate states that he died on 18th June 1878, aged 42, in 31 Birley St, Blackpool. His cause of death was *morbus cordis et pulmonum myelitis paralysis* (heart & lung problems). He also suffered from gout, which may account for the fact that he was buried in his woollen stockings.

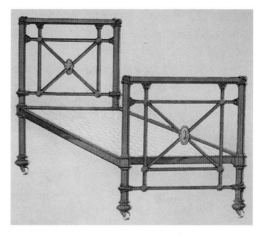

Example of the type of bedstead manufactured by the firm of 'Hulse and Haines'.

Campbell Lloyd Haines' old, heavily worn and darned woollen stockings were one of the most curious finds from the excavation at St. Martin's, especially given his prosperous background. Dye analysis showed that they were multicoloured – red toes, green up to the ankle then blue above. Sideways stretching of the stockings suggested they had covered a very sturdy calf (although post-mortem swelling is another likely cause of stretching), and they were darned at the ankle and toe, probably as a result of wear from a high-ankled boot or shoe. The style of the stockings is one that was popular

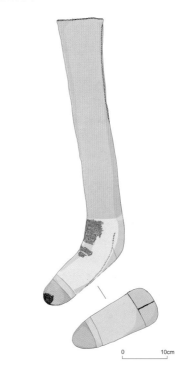

0   10cm

A schematic drawing of Campbell Lloyd Haines' woollen stockings. Note the areas of heavy darning.

in the early Victorian period, so they were more than a little old fashioned when Campbell died. Can you tell a man from his socks? Campbell's stockings and medical history suggest an overweight, unwell and rather eccentric man, and there is something about him that seems a little tragic. Was he buried in his stockings – a most unusual thing to do – because he never took them off in life, and they permanently sheathed his swollen and agonisingly painful gout-ridden legs?

Unlikely revolutionaries

In this book we have traced the development of Birmingham from an unremarkable market town of the 12th century to the manufacturing giant of the 19th century. Many books have told this story before but we have been able to adopt a unique perspective, one based primarily on the archaeological evidence. Before the Bull Ring excavations funded by The Birmingham Alliance, it was simply not possible to adopt this perspective – no major excavations had taken place. Although necessarily fragmentary, the archaeological evidence for manufacturing, from the leather industry of the medieval period through to the brass industry of the 18th century, has played a large role in our account. And we have seen how, in the 18th century, there was a transformation in the archaeological record of the town, which corresponds to its transformation into what Arthur Young in 1791 called 'the first manufacturing town in the world'.

To call Birmingham 'the first manufacturing town in the world' is quite a claim. It gives Birmingham a pre-eminent position in a revolution that has affected the world more profoundly than any other episode in human history. And who were the revolutionaries? We can claim with some justification that they were the men and women buried in St. Martin's churchyard. Unlikely revolutionaries, certainly, and unknown to us as individuals until the archaeological excavations cast a small shaft of light into their tombs. In an important sense they are just ordinary middle-class people – an ironmonger, a chemist, a saddler – whose lives were beset by the joys and griefs of ordinary living (the joy of the birth of a child and the grief of an early death are aspects that come through strongly from the evidence that we have). But we are also struck by certain patterns.

Many of those whose lives we have traced were immigrants who came into Birmingham from various parts of the Midlands to make their fortune – for example the Warden and Browett families from villages in the Coventry area, John Sansom from Bilston in Staffordshire, Hannah Ainsworth from Inkberrow in Worcestershire (and their domestic servants were likewise often immigrants). Here they swelled the mushrooming population of the town and did, indeed, make their fortune. A typical pattern is of starting off a business in one of the old parts of Birmingham around the Bull Ring, where one lived over the shop, and then expanding and diversifying the business until one could afford to move out to a house in fashionable Edgbaston or Harborne. Another pattern – so obvious that it might easily be overlooked – is that they made their fortune by and large in making and selling things. In the handful of lives we have briefly examined, only two – the soldier and the lawyer – do not fall into this pattern, and if we had examined further examples the pattern would have been reinforced. Amongst those we have not so far mentioned are Joseph Warden (junior), a maker of carriage and gig springs, Alfred Browett (junior), a silversmith, William Jenkins, a brass founder, and Thomas and Leonard Jenkins, wire manufacturers – all representative Birmingham trades.

Finally, at the end of their lives these successful manufacturers and their relatives were buried in a vault at St. Martin's that symbolised their success in life and marked them and their families off from the less fortunate. Of course, the very fact that they were buried in these vaults introduces a bias – these were by definition the successful families. Those whose businesses failed, those who died in the workhouse, are amongst the many more numerous, anonymous, burials in the earth-cut graves. However, the bulk of these anonymous burials are no doubt of working-class men, women and children – those who actually made the 'patent railway spikes and boiler rivets; anvils, vices, hammers, tue irons, bellows, screw and wind-up jacks; spades, shovels, tyre springs, iron arms, axle-trees, hurdles, chains, hames, chains, files, nails, &c., &c.' manufactured at Joseph Warden & Sons' Edgbaston Street premises. To approach their lives through archaeology our best bets are the study of their physical remains, with its promise of details on health and diet, and the excavation of the places of work themselves – the excavations at Edgbaston Street and Park Street (although relating in the main to earlier periods) showed the potential. The future for archaeology in the first manufacturing town in the world is full of exciting possibilities.

To describe the men and women buried in St. Martin's churchyard as 'revolutionaries' will certainly seem to some an unlikely proposition. It is undoubtedly true that most of those whose names we have uncovered were active not in the first stage of the Industrial Revolution, in the late 18th century, but in its later stages and beyond. Nevertheless, the Revolution was created, however unwittingly, by people like them. Who else can be credited with it? Certainly not the statesmen, nobility and established gentry, who generally struggled to adapt to events rather than shaping them. Nor, being realistic, the mass of working people who similarly adapted to circumstances and took employment where it could best be found.

The classic image of the Industrial Revolution is of Lancashire cotton mills – 'dark, satanic mills' – and terrible exploitation of workers in huge factories with water- or steam-driven machinery. In Birmingham the story is different, although we should not underestimate the appalling conditions in which some of the working

The 21st-century Bullring – a very Birmingham thing.

class lived and worked. Here the 'revolution', if this is the right word, was driven mainly it seems by numerous small- and medium-sized businesses making use of relatively simple – but nevertheless highly effective – hand technology. Emblematic of such small- and, as his business developed, medium-sized concerns is that of Joseph Warden, iron, steel and tin plate merchant.

The phenomenon known as the Industrial Revolution was a complex web of interacting forces where it can be very difficult to distinguish cause from effect. However, a 'manufacturing revolution' was not possible without a concomitant 'consumer revolution' – manufactures need a market. It is appropriate, therefore, that the Bull Ring archaeological excavations were occasioned by the development of a retail complex – Bullring – aimed at creating a new consumer experience. From Peter de Birmingham to the present, such innovation is a very 'Birmingham thing'.

Notes

Chapter 3

Pages 25-33   *Moor Street and Park Street boundary ditch interpreted as a watercourse.* Stephanie Rátkai, the pottery specialist, is uncomfortable with the interpretation of this ditch as a watercourse. The pottery, she observes, shows no signs of prolonged immersion in water and the environmental evidence suggests still or slow-flowing water at best. However, the deposition of the pottery and the environmental data relate mainly to the disuse of the ditch. This issue will be discussed more fully in the monograph publication.

Chapter 4

Page 49   *The Hersum Ditch.* The arguments concerning the identification of the Hersum Ditch with the large boundary ditch uncovered on the excavations at the Moor Street and Park Street sites is complex. In his forthcoming article 'The Hersum Ditch, Birmingham and Coventry: a Local Topographical Term?' in *Transactions of the Birmingham and Warwickshire Archaeological Society*, George Demidowicz presents the documentary evidence (from property deeds) in detail. The objection that the ditch recorded in documentary references, which range in date from 1341 to 1681, cannot be the ditch found in the excavations because the excavations show that the ditch was filled in before the references begin can be countered. Demidowicz argues that following the laying out of Moor Street and Park Street '… the ditch would have become redundant and would have formed a convenient repository for rubbish. It is probable that the water continued streaming down the hill within a small open channel or 'gutter' in levels, now removed, above and roughly on the line of the filled-in ditch'.

Page 50   *Date of laying out of Moor Street and Park Street.* Stephanie Rátkai, the pottery specialist, favours an earlier – 12th-century – date for the laying out of Moor Street and Park Street than that given here. She does so on the grounds that small quantities of 12th-century pottery were found at both the Moor Street and Park Street sites, suggesting activity prior to the 13th century. The presence of this 12th-century pottery may be interpreted in other ways, however. The issue will be discussed further in the monograph publication.

Page 50   *Origins of Deritend market.* I am grateful to Dr Richard Holt for the observation about the possibility that the market at Deritend was originally founded by the lords of Aston and subsequently taken over by the lords of Birmingham.

Further Reading and Information

The archaeological excavations described in this book were the first major investigations to be carried out in Birmingham city centre. However, development across Birmingham continues apace and many other excavations have taken place in recent years. The whole story of Birmingham's archaeology from prehistory to the present will be told in a book to be published in 2004:

Hodder, Mike forthcoming *Birmingham: The Hidden History*, Tempus.

Full academic accounts of the excavations described in this book will be published in 2004 by Oxbow Books as *The Bull Ring Uncovered* and *St. Martin's Uncovered*.

The following books provide accessible, up-to-date accounts of Birmingham's history up to the 19th century and sometimes beyond. Most are in print and reasonably priced. Note that where Carl Chinn says in *One Thousand Years of Brum*, page 28, that 10th-century pottery had been found in the vicinity of the Bull Ring, this was based on rumours in 1999 that pre-Conquest pottery had been found on the Edgbaston Street site described in this book. As it turned out, the rumours were without foundation.

Chinn, Carl 1999 *One Thousand Years of Brum*, Birmingham Evening Mail.

Holt, Richard 1985 *The Early History of the Town of Birmingham 1166 to 1600*, Dugdale Society Occasional Paper No.30.

Hopkins, Eric 1989 *Birmingham: The First Manufacturing Town in the World, 1760-1840*, Weidenfield & Nicholson. (Also published as *The Rise of the Manufacturing Town: Birmingham and the Industrial Revolution*, 1998, Sutton.)

Leather, Peter 2001 *A Brief History of Birmingham*, Brewin Books.

Skipp, Victor 1980 *A History of Greater Birmingham – down to 1830*. (New edition 1997, Brewin Books.)

Skipp, Victor 1983 *The Making of Victorian Birmingham*. (New edition 1996, Brewin Books.)

Upton, Chris 1993 *A History of Birmingham*, Phillimore.

Although hardly up-to-date, William Hutton's *History of Birmingham*, first published in 1781 with several subsequent editions, makes entertaining and informative reading, full of amusing comments on the Birmingham of his day. When Hutton writes of Birmingham's earlier history he remains entertaining but is wholly unreliable.

For full details on the 1970s salvage excavations on the Birmingham Moat:

Watts, Lorna 1980 'Birmingham Moat: its history, topography and destruction', *Transactions of the Birmingham & Warwickshire Archaeological Society* Vol. 89, 1-77.

If the excavation of St. Martin's Churchyard have stimulated you, an excellent general account of the English funeral is:

Litten, Julian 1991 *The English Way of Death: the Common Funeral since 1450.* (New edition 2002, Robert Hale.)

For a general account of the English middle classes during the period represented by the burials in the brick-lined graves and vaults at St. Martin's:

Davidoff, Leonore and Hall, Catherine 1987 *Family Fortunes: Men and Women of the English Middle Class 1780-1850* (New edition 2002, Routledge).

One aim of this book has been not only to describe the results of the archaeological excavations in advance of the construction of Bullring but also to explain how archaeologists go about their work. Two introductory books which explore this in more detail are:

Greene, Kevin 2002 *Archaeology: an Introduction* (4th edition), Routledge.

Robinson, Tony and Aston, Mick 2003 *Archaeology is Rubbish: A Beginners Guide*, Channel 4 Books.

If you want to keep abreast of archaeological discoveries in Birmingham and the west Midlands, the Council for British Archaeology (CBA) publishes an annual round up in *West Midlands Archaeology*. For details of joining the CBA contact: Council for British Archaeology, Bowes Morrell House, 111 Walmgate, York, YO1 2UA. *01904 671417*

The City Council also maintains web pages on Birmingham's archaeology: www.birmingham.gov.uk/archaeology.

More detailed articles on Birmingham's archaeology and history appear in the *Transactions of the Birmingham & Warwickshire Archaeological Society*. For information about the society write to: Birmingham & Warwickshire Archaeological Society, c/o Birmingham and Midland Institute, Margaret Street, Birmingham, B3 3BS.

Index

About the Author

Simon Buteux BA MPhil MIFA was born in Sutton Coldfield and studied archaeology at the Universities of Birmingham and Cambridge. He has carried out numerous excavations in Britain and abroad. He was for many years a Director of *Birmingham Archaeology* and a tutor in archaeology at the University of Birmingham's Centre for Lifelong Learning. He is currently Divisional Leader for Archaeology and Heritage Management in the University's Institute of Archaeology and Antiquity.